# JAMIL ALBUQUERQUE

# The art of dealing with
# PEOPLE

**THE ART OF DEALING WITH PEOPLE**

Copyright © 2004 by Jamil Albuquerque

ISBN: 978-1-64095-628-5

Ebook ISBN: 978-1-64095-629-2

All rights reserved: Citadel Editorial SA

*The contents of this book are the sole responsibility of the author and do not necessarily reflect the views of the publisher.*

**Editorial production and distribution:**

contato@citadel.com.br
www.citadel.com.br

Distributed in English language by:

SOUND WISDOM

P.O. Box 310 · Shippensburg, PA 17257-0310 · 717-530-2122

info@soundwisdom.com

1 2025

# JAMIL ALBUQUERQUE

# The art of dealing with
# PEOPLE

I dedicate this book to my family.

# SUMMARY

**Preface** .................................................................. 11

**No one can cross their time alone** ........................................ 15
    An informal education for business and life ............................... 17
    Emotions and business.................................................. 19
    Hard starts model strong people ........................................ 22
    The proposal........................................................... 26
    I believe in method .................................................... 28
    The tale of 'the cat jump' ............................................. 29
    Why am I saying all this now?........................................... 30
    What is intelligence?................................................... 31
    The intelligence and its types ......................................... 32
    Interpersonal intelligence ............................................. 36

# PART I

**How to make people like you more** .................................................. 39

    Diamond fields .................................................................................. 39

    World Citizens ................................................................................. 40

    Have a pleasant personality ........................................................ 41

    Stop being grouchy ........................................................................ 43

    Business ............................................................................................ 47

    Stop trying to model others ........................................................ 49

    Control the criticism .................................................................... 52

    Have a smile in your face ............................................................ 56

    Be cordial to people ..................................................................... 59

    Pay attention to details ............................................................... 61

    Talk about what matters to the other person and listen carefully ........................................................ 76

    Do something different, something that adds value ............. 81

    Value the other person and do it sincerely ............................. 85

    Summary of part one .................................................................... 86

# PART II

**How to influence people** .................................................. 91

    How? ........................................................................... 92

    The power in the art of influencing ........................... 98

    Be diplomatic ........................................................... 101

    Start in a friendly way ............................................. 104

    Learn to ask questions ............................................. 105

    Techniques for asking questions ............................. 106

    Be sympathetic to the other person's ideas ............ 111

    Understand and respect the opinion of others ....... 114

    Human Connection of Principles ........................... 116

    Command with skill ................................................ 117

    Communication ....................................................... 119

    Power and authority ................................................ 120

    Realize the situation ................................................. 120

    Surprise the other people by praising them ........... 122

    Have an appreciation instinct ................................. 125

    Sell your ideas in a dramatized way ....................... 128

    Know how to launch challenges with skill ............ 130

    If necessary, step back ............................................. 132

    Be tolerant ................................................................ 136

    A good example ....................................................... 137

Remember: scolding is the tool of those unprepared..............139

Summary of part two........................................................140

# PART III

**How to deal with difficult people and manage conflicts .......143**

High-performance leadership......................................................143

Focus on something good on the person first .....................147

Avoid unnecessary discussions and problems.........................149

Ask questions that lead to the solution .......................................151

Avoid sharply pointing errors ........................................154

Allow the other person to try again ..............................................155

Encourage, when progress is made................................157

Admit that you also make mistakes .............................................159

Remember the three "R's" .............................................................160

Give a person a good reputation ..................................................164

Be polite and firm in commanding the process .......................166

Conclusion ....................................................................171

Bibliography ........................................................................143

# PREFACE

We live in times where technological stress, competitiveness, a sense of urgency to make things happen, the valuation of having and the overload of activities have been the keynote.

We have taken an unprecedented leap in technology. We talk about atoms we'll never see and planets we'll never step on. But, paradoxically, we have not carved out the grounds of our psyche, nor do we know how to talk about our most intimate experiences, such as our dreams, projects, frustrations, fears, daring blows.

We become existential passersby, people who go through life without trying to understand it minimally. We do not realize how brief is our existence, the importance of our interpersonal relationships, the art of contemplating the beautiful, the ability to notice small events in our daily routine, such as the scent of flowers, a birdsong, the beauty of a sunset or the magnitude of a simple dialogue.

Our time is barely enough for our social and professional activities and day-to-day responsibilities.

The human development is the door that opens only from the inside. We have to change our intimate view so that a new sun can rise in our day.

It is very easy to invest in machinery and equipment. It is very easy, for example, to set up an orchestra. It is enough to have money. Instruments are bought, musicians are hired, but tuning the orchestra and having "music poets" capable of reading the score and playing the melody as a unique work requires leadership, sensitivity, skills, study, and preparation.

So today, the big challenge is to prepare people.

The proposal that Jamil, with objectiveness and competence, brings in his book is exactly this one - preparing people, building relationships, crossing psychic worlds. Teach "how to do" so that people can work out an inner alchemy, transforming their behavior, observing details and putting simple things into practice, but that makes a huge difference.

It is up to each one to allow himself to be penetrated by the teachings contained here. The secret is to hold the direction of our lives in our hands and develop skills to be the authors of our stories.

We must place ourselves as eternal learners before life, rethinking our paradigms, renewing our values and concepts. Let yourself be guided through the pages of this book and get aboard for the journey proposed by Jamil to improve your interpersonal intelligence.

**Augusto Cury**

We must place ourselves as eternal learners before life, rethinking our paradigms, renewing our values and concepts. Let yourself be guided through the pages of this book and get aboard for the journey proposed by [illegible] interpersonal intelligence.

Augusto Cury

# NO ONE CAN CROSS THEIR TIME ALONE

▶ ▶ ▶ ▶ ▶ ▶ ▶ ▶ ▶ ▶

Successful relationships have been one of the greatest enigmas of modernity and this is also increasingly important in corporate life. In a recent survey performed with American millionaires, they chose relationships as one of the main factors that helped them achieve financial success. It is not the equity, nor bonds, the value criterion of the very wealthy on Wall Street, but people. And everyone is unanimous in stating that interpersonal relationships are not a field of innocence. But, certainly, a field of diplomacy.

The lack of skill in human relationships does not only affect marriage, dating or friendship; it also affects professional, political, business and even international relationships. That is, the way a successful person relates to his friends, family, and customers is what makes the difference. But this our time is a different time, we have cell phones, the internet, emails and social networks that are everywhere. Performing tasks just got easier and faster. Paradoxically, it added a sense of urgency to our lives. Urgency brings stress and we all know that in highly stressed environments, the potential for conflict between people grows exponentially. So, in these times of intelligent organizations, participatory leadership, learning communities, engagement and commitment, companies that learn, "hierarchy-broken" structures - we could say so – to develop the ability to sell ideas and gain cooperation is of vital importance for building a prosperous career and developing effective leadership.

Human relationship. This is fundamentally what this book is about.

*To exist is to interact with!*

The human being is sociable by nature, the human being was born to live in groups. And to live in groups, rules must be followed. Rules govern groups and groups govern the world. Although there is no established formula that presents equal results for everyone - as is the case with some sciences - human relations are an art: And since the times before Christ, human beings have already needed to understand this art. Even in art, which requires a lot of inspiration and talent, there are techniques. And we know that techniques, principles, and formulas make life easier and increase effectiveness.

## 1. An informal education for business and life

There are two situations in the professional life: we either have results, or we have excuses! And if we were as good at delivering results as we are skillful at making excuses, we would make a revolution within the group in which we belong. The result is consequent - it results from something. We present here in this book the secret of the manual. It is a formidable material, but not new; simple, but not easy, but certainly achievable. These are obvious things that we ignore, that when put into practice, have great results. The great paradox is that common and practical things rarely translate into common practices.

Cássio Seixas, HR director at Rodobens, once explained that, although the reader - like many participants in the Master Mind Lince course - may think "I already knew that", when reflecting on his ability to applying this intellectual knowledge, he will prove that "knowing that" is very different from "knowing how". Our purpose is to help you, the reader, find this internal information and turn it into an application in real-world behavior, as the useful knowledge is knowing how, not knowing that. Information is a necessary condition, although insufficient, to achieve effectiveness in action. The difference between theory and practice is summarized in a word: ACTION, which is close to the initiative. To take advantage of this text, you must get involved with it, read it with a pencil in hand, agreeing, discussing, inquiring, connecting ideas with experiences and concrete situations in your life. Read, check, reread until you enter "the autopilot of the mind". The ideas are deceptively simple, instrumental, so they look easy. In fact, there are revolutionary principles, practices, and philosophies hidden in this text. What seems common sense in the first reading, in the second or third, opens up as a fascinating possibility for individual and cultural improvement. Once, Osvaldo Caproni, an entrepreneur, president of COACAVO, Votuporanga, SP, a master at the University of São Paulo - USP, told me: "Jamil, when these tools are applied with skill, they are like a white weapon, so effective they are".

That's why I recommend that you don't just stick on the first reading or the first impression.

## Why don't we see the obvious?

Because the obvious is like the air. Not noticeable to us. In the same way that the fish does not perceive the water. Only when it is taken out of the water. We only perceive the air when we dive our head into the water. That is, in the absence. Likewise, human relationships, when everything is well, seem so normal that, sometimes, we don't even feel the need to care for them. That is why, at times, we are so harsh with people we love, they are so present in our lives that we don't even realize it. But, in the absence, "we ran out of air".

## 2. Emotions and businesses

What distinguished successful people from medians is the way they deal with their emotions and especially with other people. The more closed the person is by his temperament, in his heart, there will always be, to a greater or lesser extent, this basic, elementary need for human contact.

Managing tangible assets within an intangible economy, as the intellectual capital is, is the competitive advantage of leadership. Companies are rigid institutions, tangible entities. The people who are part of it, who make up its structure, are the ones who give it life, those which pulsate, which gives it dynamism. The more improved the communication between these people, the greater their productivity. At the end of the experience, when the people of the company go home, the company goes too.

Dorival Balbino, from Ribeirão Preto, who started as a salesman of socks and is now a great businessman, often says: "If you want to grow, you have to know how to compose, because the difference in a company is the people". Today, his company is one of the largest in Latin America in the balloon business.

Mário Spaniol, the creator of Carmen Steffens trademark of women's shoes, a 'gaucho' – a man from Rio Grande do Sul - from Franca and who produces the shoe that is the object of women's desire, once told me:

"We have to get away from that rooted and backward concept that the company is good, the product is good, the mission is great ... what spoils are the people."

The quality of products generated by a company is directly related to the quality of communication and the relationship between the people who compose it. A 100% company is not built with 50% of people.

In a survey, William Glasser, an American organizational consultant, says that finances, statistics, flowcharts, and high technology are essential to running a successful company, but companies do not break for lack of this technological knowledge: its failure has to do with people.

## People: the energy that binds the company!

Companies that go bankruptcy seem unable to learn that people fail to operate effectively, not because they are incompetent in the technical aspects of their tasks, but because of the way they are treated by their leaders and how they treat others. A survey shows that 87% of organizations that go bankruptcy due to the individual attitudes of the people in charge, their temperaments, the way they relate and their inability to lead teams. That is, most companies go bankruptcy not by the market, but by people.

Visualize the importance of developing the ability to manage your company's intellectual capital in this age of knowledge.

Because salary cannot buy the team spirit.

Only skills can do that.

Whatever a person's professional occupation, he can immediately put into practice all the principles contained herein. This book is the synthesis and expression of the common sense, of what has already worked and what I have been told by several people in my long journey of personal development, research, my own experience, and my preferred authors. For this reason, you, the reader, will find the reference from a successful company, entrepreneur or professional many times. I do this for two reasons: the first is to give credit to the author of the idea, and the second, so you can realize that they are people as common as you or me and that, if they were successful, it was thanks to the courage to develop skills inherent to any of us.

Accept my sincere congratulations, because if you have come this far in this book, it is because you have a real desire to develop this skill in dealing with people. And this is the first step of a great journey.

## 3. Hard starts model strong people

What matters to the world is not how much you have gone through to achieve your goals. What really matters is how much you have achieved.

However, to know how we've reached our goals, it is important to know which ways have been followed.

It is like inviting a person to enter the back door of your home; for it is there that you expose yourself and show what you are, or when you ask the guest to go to the kitchen to see the preparation of the meal, before serving the ready supper in the dining room. Make yourself known. Leon Tolstoy, a Russian writer, said that, if you want to speak to the world, speak of your village. In a parody to this great thinker, I want to share my journey from the village I was born to until building-up my knowledge. And this is what I share here, in summary.

My parents professed an extremely rigid religious faith, based on Protestant Christian fundamentalism, and we, the children, were raised with this ingrained conviction as a background. I am the sixth child in a family of ten brothers who lived on a minimum wage, as settlers on a farm, located near a village called Monte Carlo, in the western side of Santa Catarina. In the 1960s, the region had just over 50 families, surviving on the extraction of the araucaria pine around a sawmill. A common history, similar to that of millions of Brazilians, since Brazil was an agricultural country that was urbanized after the 1960s of the 20th century, and the whole world was with one foot in the fields and another in the city.

We were brought up within the narrow limits of this austerity of vision and under a strong hand. It was the way my parents found to raise ten children, as was the custom at that time. In addition to this hard, arduous, laborious life, requiring huge efforts, another ghost stubbornly hovered around me, frightening, fearful: my natural bashfulness, a reluctant shyness. A legacy of the kind of family orientation to which I was subjected and the high severity of the religious house I attended to. In this way, I was molded like an ashamed type, turned to myself, closed like an oyster trapped inside the shell.

Shy people are usually great for others, but terrible for themselves. Thus, shyness, a constant enemy, was the obstacle to be overcome. That seemed to be an insurmountable barrier, eternally present in my contacts with others. Talking to people was a real torture for me. I admired people who had this facility - fluent speech in front of others.

My mother taught me to read with the Bible and that was my first contact with the culture. This was my first big difference, because when I entered school, I already knew how to read, which, at that time and in that agricultural region was something rare. This, in a way, modeled my character and helped me develop a taste for reading.

### I had and I have in the Bible my inexhaustible source of knowledge!

A frequent visitor to public libraries, I read everything that appeared before me: from a medicine leaflet to novels by famous authors. Even Karl Marx's Capital, I read it before I turned 15. I was a real "bookworm". But one reading in particular, when I was 14 years old, had a significant effect on my life and worked as the beginning of a new moment. At that time, I lived in Balneário Camboriú, SC, where we moved with my older brother, married, who already lived on the coast. It was The Law of Triumph by Napoleon Hill. This book, known worldwide and one of the 30 most read and studied books in the world after the Holy Bible, an epic of the science of behavior, was published in 1928 and had such a strong impact on me that it guides up to now my way of life. It shows that triumph is the integration of all the roles of life. At home, in business, with friends and in corporate life. It shows the human side of success, triumph and success. From theory to practice it was a leap. I had just finished reading the book and I was already filling myself with hope, ready to put into action what I had learned.

> Scalation started right there until
> I became the person I am today.

I managed to advance in my school education, specializing in architecture. In this area, I was outstanding.

Some of my works have become page-time in some Brazilian cities, and I keep them in my files with great pride. I moved on, completing university education courses in the areas of business administration, economics and marketing. I pursued an academic career, without losing sight of my basic, essential vocation, of seeking development in the art of human relationships, including making a long foray into behavioral therapy. In this area of human development, I invested a lot of my life, knowing and studying all the methods, programs, systems, designs and sequence of events of the courses existing in the market, including becoming an instructor and advisor of several processes of personal development. In particular, I became a Master Mind Instructor for the Napoleon Hill

Foundation, based in Indiana, USA. I also became a visiting professor at the University of California (UCSD), USA, for the global leadership course, specialist in city management, professor of graduate studies at Faap, of the city manager course, I held government positions, mentored great business and public leaders. Much of what we learned together I write here in this book.

A biography "is never the truth, nothing but the truth", as the great poet Carlos Drummond de Andrade used to say; "all the facts are actually two: itself and its version". Overall, I think I synthesized the journey.

## 4. The proposal

Observing the behavior of people within the scope of corporate organizations and the impressions and images that they evidence wherever they go, I realized that some leave indelible marks, while others not so much.

This experience allowed me to conclude that the ability to express oneself and the quality of interpersonal relationships are the differential between someone's failure and success in the exercise of their professional activity.

In the midst of this activity, I had the privilege of living with very interesting people, some of whom are now part of my circle of friends.

One of these friends, Eduardo Mendes, a former Municipal Secretary of Culture of Ribeirão Preto and one of the creators of the Ribeirão Preto Book Fair, the largest in the open air in the country, and today coordinator of the Ibero-American Year of Reading, suggested me to transform into a book, everything I talk about in the Master Mind training, with current examples, closer to Brazilian reality and culture. He said to me:

> *Jamil, when you are going to explain the law of success of a pleasant personality, do it with such enthusiasm, affection and dedication that you need to record it in a book. Write it down for people to read the examples during the course and after it, in any quadrant of this immense nation that is Brazil. The vast majority of books in this area have examples from people from other countries and today there is already a Brazilian reality, a 21st century Brazilian professional, which needs to be valued more. Real people, not myths and of distant proof.*

I bought the idea and decided to tell what I hear in training rooms - and outside them - of ordinary people, who decided to live a life above mediocrity and invested in their personal development. From this aquifer, the inspiration for my idea of creating and transforming this project into reality. Something that could serve as a guide, a script, a compass for those who are keenly interested in being instrumentalized, to join the list of people skilled in the art of dealing with others. Before being a book, The Art of Dealing with People was a seminar, so this kind of spoken way of writing, as if it were a lecture. While reading, listen as if you were watching me speak and feeling the variables of a training room on leadership, interpersonal intelligence and effective communication.

## 5. I believe in method

The Greek word Meta means target. Method means a path to the target! The person, when he has a goal and a method, has a minimum that allows him to advance beyond the target. The method allows the person to have a super-advance, a break barriers. Why? **The method organizes and enhances knowledge**. The method is a mode of action. And the method is what allows ordinary people to do something that was once accomplished by brilliant minds. The method organizes, potentializes and systematizes, step by step, what a very skilled individual has learned to overcome. A dwarf can see farther than a giant, as long as he climbs on the giant's shoulders. **The method is the giant!** But he must be humble to recognize that he sees further because the giant lent his shoulders. That is why we respect the Master Mind method, which gives human beings extraordinary tooling empowerment.

## 6. The tale of the 'Cat Jump'

Whenever I conduct sales seminars, I hear new salespeople comment that old ones never teach the 'cat jump'.

to the new generation. They 'hold something back', as they say in their slang. The legend has it that the expression "the cat jump" came about because there was a tiger in the forest that wanted to eat the cat. As always, when the tiger made the attempt, the cat would make its extraordinary leaps, and the tiger never managed to catch the cat. One day, the tiger had a brilliant idea. It hired the cat to train it the art of jumping. The cat spent the entire month training the tiger, teaching all the jumps it knew. At the end of training, the tiger paid the cat royally for the services provided. While the cat was counting the money, the tiger thought: Now I know all its jumps and I will relish it. The tiger jumped over the cat. The cat went off on a tangent and jumped on a tree branch, leaving the tiger gaping. With a silly face, the tiger asked: Wait, you didn't teach me this jump!!!??? The cat then gave it the answer that would become famous: Not this one. This is the 'cat jump'!

## How is the cat jump like?

The cat, regardless of how high it jumps, always falls with its four legs down. It doesn't matter if it's three meters or ten meters. Formula 1 racing experts have been studying this cat's ability to react so quickly.

They realized that when the cat falls, it immediately puts its face horizontally in relation to the floor and its tail pointed upwards, so this allows it to be able to turn its body on itself, with unusual speed. You can throw the cat upwards two hundred times as it will always use the same principle to fall upright. That is, the cat has a method! Which leads us to believe that cat jumping is the method!

Formula 1 teams train their drivers in this way. When at 300 kilometers per hour, they realize they are going to hit, they turn their faces to the side, and this allows them to divert attention away from the obstacle, and often, at 300 kilometers per hour, to avoid accidents. They use the cat method, blur to not hit.

## 7. Why am I saying all this now?

Because on the following pages you will find a method for dealing with people. You will find here the three steps of execution: What? How? And the action. What is the knowledge.

How is the strategy. Action is the strength and that is up to you. You will find here in this book how to make people like you, enjoy life more, create networks of contacts, expand your ability to multiply results through people and interpersonal intelligence.

## 8. What is intelligence?

Scholars say it is "a skill, sharpness, mental insight". Professors say it is "the ability to convert abstract phenomena". Psychologists say it is "the capacity for perception, understanding, learning and adaptation. In other words, the capacity for adaptability". Poets say that intelligence "is to be happy". In the business world, it is said that "intelligence is the ability to use mental skills and transform them into benefits". It is a utilitarian view, typical of business. A little strong, but it shows that the human being has responsibility for his mental quality. Intelligence is the interconnection of ideas. It is the ability to access knowledge at any time. Intelligence is the active function of the soul, as well as feeling and will. It is from this organic-spiritual gear that the skills of thinking and acting are born. And this is what makes the human being superior to animals, because from the extension of his conceptions he deduces that his activity will be greater and more productive when applied to the social welfare of all. Therefore, intelligence is not a privilege, it is a responsibility. But it always rewards us for the demand it causes us. The word responsibility, if divided into two parts, becomes response and skill. Responsibility requires skillful responses. It is to what Interpersonal Intelligence is proposed.

## 9. The intelligence and its types

Can it be said that a person is intelligent in some aspects of life, but not in others? It seems so. At the beginning of the last century, the American psychologist L.L. Thurstone, who became famous in the academic world as a great test designer, stated that there are several types of intelligence and therefore, not all people can be qualified based on the same size.

But it was the American psychologist Howard Gardner, a specialist in cognition and education at Harvard University, who shed more light on the issue. In 1978, he published the book Multiple Intelligences, highlighting a new way of thinking about the previously closed question of intelligence.

According to Gardner, three aspects are important:

①— We are endowed with several intelligences.
②— All intelligences are present in all people, but with quantitative differences.
③— All intelligences can be increased through the use.

We are facing a new reality, especially when it is said that the different types of intelligence can be increased through use. The famous law of use and disuse of French biologist Monet Lamarck. Use develops, not use atrophy! All parts of the body react in the same way, including the brain. Clearly, the brain will not grow anatomically, but its synapses, which are the connections between neurons, or nerve cells, which improve the functional capacity of the brain, may have increased. This is achieved with the individual stimulation of each intelligence.

Gardner referred to the existence of seven intelligences so cataloged:

① – Logical-mathematical intelligence.
② – Linguistic intelligence.
③ – Musical intelligence.
④ – Spatial intelligence.
⑤ – Interpersonal intelligence.
⑥ – Intrapersonal intelligence.
⑦ – Kinesthetic body intelligence.

The person who trains one more than the other has better results in that area of most interest.

In Brazil, psychiatrist Augusto Cury has also been researching and studying intelligence for over two decades. He developed a theory called Multifocal Intelligence.

In this theory, he studies the four great processes of building intelligence, namely:

①— The construction of thoughts.
②— The transformation of emotional energy.
③— The formation of intrapsychic history stored in the memory.
④— The formation of existential awareness.

Cury, in his research, realized that the world seeks people who:

- are the authors of their history;
- are life-changing agents;
- know how to manage their thoughts and manage their emotion;
- are safe, creative leaders, capable of seeking solutions with a wider range of psychic tools.

People with improved determination and discipline so that, in these times of competitiveness and sense of urgency, they can withstand pressure without "stripping the screw threads", as they say in the slang.

And then, the question arises: is it possible to strengthen more fragile facets of a person's intelligence? Research shows that it does. There are no immediate formulas or magic wands. This is what exists:

*The determination of making progress*

The willpower to develop personally is the sword that makes human beings win the war against stagnation. Dr. Daniel Goleman, a notable American psychologist, also from Harvard University, has released an interesting book on emotional intelligence. He gathered in one volume everything that had been said in the world about personal and professional development and proved, through researches, that people endowed with great intellectual skill, a lot of culture and technical knowledge, they often find themselves defeated by the emotional aspect, an extremely human weakness. Goleman, at the beginning of his book, quotes Aristotle:

> *Anyone can get angry, that's easy. But hanging out with the right person, at the right time, for the right reason and in the right way – that's not easy.*

This Greek philosopher's thought is the purest expression of the truth. How many times we don't blow up at people we love. Often, when we blow up at our family, we are blowing up at the world. We blow up in the wrong place.

Traditional schools do not teach with an emphasis on self-knowledge, feelings management, self-motivation and skills in interpersonal relationships.

This book aims to supply a part of the continuing education, necessary for anyone involved with the business world and with the rise in their careers, emphasizing the skills in interpersonal relationships. Because knowledge is only 15% of the result of a person's triumph; 85% is what the person does with their knowledge.

## 10. Interpersonal Intelligence

In decades following careers as a coach of leaders, researching cases of results of people involved in the business world, it is possible to perceive that this intelligence is the difference between a successful professional and an average professional. It is the ability to give to each one according to their needs.

A situational leader acts according to the situation. It is neither good nor bad, it is fair. Interpersonal intelligence, when used well, has profound wisdom, as it superimposes intelligence on emotions. When misused, it can be a chaos. It is what makes the human being able to put into practice the concept of the right time and right place. The person becomes a master of his emotions.

## Applied Interpersonal Intelligence

The power of human relationships arises from the ability to recognize emotions in others, using this information as a guide for behavior and for building and maintaining relationships.

It is the "manager" of the other intelligences. It is the one that makes maturity evident and transparent in the person. It is intelligence that creates sociability, Social Intelligence! When we study the lives of all the great winners and achievers, those who have had the greatest influence on other people and made things happen, we find a similar pattern. In addition to persistence and inner struggle, they have used this intelligence skillfully, as it is a unifier.

The businessperson, when he puts this intelligence in his favor, improves his experience in diplomatic relations.

## Social Skill

A businessperson must be an artist in the knowledge of organizing relations with the different agents in his social, commercial and business context. This is the fundamental point of the economic operator, or of a great psychologist: knowing how to win people. It cannot be expected that they be the ones to recognize our nobility. Placing others in an obligation to understand us is a childish claim. It means being a loser.

How to expand this intelligence is what we are going to implement in the next pages, with techniques, rules and principles. We will work with a method. With the jump of the cat! The principles gathered here represent a formula for developing a successful career. It is worth reflecting on them, in order to create your own set, your personal synthesis, of rules and habits, which will serve as a guide throughout your professional evolution.

PART I

# HOW TO MAKE PEOPLE LIKE YOU MORE

## 1. Diamonds Fields

We all like diamonds. According to Napoleon Hill, one of the most attended lectures in the world was "Acres of diamonds", by Russel Conwell. Diamonds are forever! If someone, when giving you a diamond stone of more or less than 200 grams - which must be a wonderful sight - instead of handing it over, "hit it in the face", as it is popularly said, it will certainly hurt you, make you bleed and make you very "angry", hurt, upset, and the act will be a source of intrigue with the other person. A treasure became an object of pain. But if, on the contrary, deliver it wrapped in velvet, you will surely be very happy, as you will be receiving a great fortune. Why am I saying this? Because the same thing happens with truths, they are priceless, but if they are "thrown in the face", instead of helping, they will hurt and, sometimes, hurt a lot! We propose to improve communication skills with clarity and emotional balance to be more pleasant and effective, able to give feedback with skill.

This should be done in a simple way, because, as Russel says in his speech, "you don't have to walk far to find a diamond mine, sometimes it is under our feet". You don't have to walk around the world to be a citizen of the world.

## 2. World Citizens

They are citizens who are distinguished by their special outlook on life, by their values, by their habits. It is a kind of identity, a distinctive factor.

Successful people seem to have a universal language, regardless of their nationality or the sector in which they operate. They are people who make themselves respected and admired for their qualities and competencies and who constitute that contingent composed of individuals known as citizens of the world.

They are the nobles of today.

The good news is that all of this - qualities and skills inherent in successful people - can be developed, can be acquired through training, commitment, dedication, and will.

The Brazilian has the advantage of being one of the friendliest people on the planet. Friendships are part of the national culture and are enjoyed all the time, as a natural part of everyday life. Making of this quality a competitive skill is our proposal.

## 3. Have a pleasant personality

The most lucid, peaceful and strong people I know, are people with a pleasant personality. As Walter Kalembach, master of personal development in São Paulo, says: "The more peaceful, the stronger the person". Pleasant people manage to bring people together around a common purpose, stimulate the spirit of cooperation, they have the ability to make people walk towards their vision, thus exercising the role of the leader. They manage to develop, as Peter Drucker used to say, the great master of contemporary management, the spirit of body in a company, which is a great competitive advantage.

Among the qualities that a person with a pleasant personality has is the ability to call others by their names. The other person's name is the most musical, sweetest, smoothest, and loudest sound that exists in any language. When you call someone by name, you are, in fact, valuing that person.

Remembering a person's name is an expression of interest. And this is an element that adds, values, because in fact, it shows the desire to remember the person behind the name. Someone's name is the key that opens his universe. The name is the great heritage of the human being. It is what he bequeaths to his offspring. Even if his material inheritance is gone, his name remains forever.

When we jump into life, in the cradle, we receive our first insignia which is a name. When we jump out of life, through the grave, what is engraved on our headstone is our name. You see, dear reader, in the two most important 'customs' of our life, cradle and grave, it is the name that stands out. So, if you want to make friends, value the other person's name; if you want to make enemies, step on the other person's name. As the focus of our work is making friends, the first big tip is: call people by their name.

There is the appreciative name, the one that the person likes most, which ends up becoming his logo. There are nicknames, which can be appreciative and derogatory. There are transfer names, those that the person receives in honor of family members, important, famous and that the person sometimes carries it with pride, sometimes less. As a leader, you have to know this in advance.

In doing so, the pleasant personality will flourish. And those who have this ability to call people by their names generate trust, attract, approach and manage to lead more easily. They leave their positive mark wherever they go.

## 4. Stop being grouchy

There are people who still reproduce a behavior inherited from our ancestors, who lived intensely in classical capitalism, in which the important thing was to generate and accumulate capital and that was the only satisfaction: in the pride of getting rich. However, enjoying life or spending money on comfort or leisure were not part of the plans; they were a waste of time and resources. In the agricultural Brazil, this reference lasted longer than in Europe and North America.

This behavior started to weaken with the modernist movement, and today the ideal of people is to be happy. But we still know people who justify themselves and apologize for enjoying some rest, on their generally incessant journey, insisting on being gruff, cold and eternally tense. These people build an altar of concerns and visit it every day, as they have learned to associate this - being concerned - with being RESPONSIBLE.

Don't take yourself too seriously. Having a healthy sense of humor is preferable - even for an executive - to being sour and concerned all the time or boasting an air of meticulous austerity. It will be much better for your blood pressure, and for team morale, to laugh in disastrous situations, instead of maintaining a tense and tragic appearance of impending catastrophe when things go wrong.

It is clear that the most serious problems must be taken seriously. Of course, employees need to behave with dignity, but maintaining a heavy and oppressive atmosphere around them will do more harm than good. One of the strongest roots of a bad mood is that you have not properly forgiven your own soul for the mistakes made at some mysterious time. Even if you don't detect these errors, forgive yourself anyway.

I remember a lecture I gave in 2003, in Fernandópolis, in the west of São Paulo, at UNATI – Universidade da Terceira Idade [University of the Third Age] -, for about 1,500 elderly people. It was a very interesting experience that we had, my friend André Soares and me. While talking with some people who started to arrive at the lecture, one of the event's organizers, Edvilson Fontana, the owner of a chain of drugstores, approached me, and addressing to me, said: "Jamil, we are going to have people today from 93 years old, 95 years old, we even have the presence of a 97 year old person". In the meantime, I was introduced to a 93-year-old man who was in a very good mood. Our conversation was about that: good mood. In his view, good mood was the spice of life. Then I met another person who recognized me and asked me, "Do you remember me?" I looked at that man who had one hand on one side, an evident lack of control over his movements, a sequel to some health problem and I then replied: "No, I don't remember, but I want to hug you". As we hugged, he told me: "I remember you from Ribeirão Preto, in a lecture at the Associação Comercial. My name is João Antunes".

"Boy, how different you are," was my spontaneous reaction. We then had a conversation. "What happened?", I asked, between surprised and curious.

"I am living here; I came here to live with my son, I'm recovering from a stroke. I'm 56 years old."

"Young man, a kid is what you look like, close to these people in here."

"Yes, but now, at 56, I am much younger than I was in 1998, when you met me."

"Why? What happened? - I asked."

"I separated from my wife after many years and soon after I had a stroke. I was a very grouchy guy. I had to experience this tragedy, I had to lose my family, I had to start all over again to realize that grouchiness had taken away from my youth to my joy of living."

"What do you mean? - I asked."

He said: "My level of demand was very high. When I got out of the car, if another vehicle was parked too close, it would ruin my day. Today I think: why not using the other door? There's the gear stick in the middle, but that's the least in comparison to my day!".

*Age brings wrinkles to skin, but grouchiness
brings wrinkles to the soul!*

Here is an example that in the adversity we discover what we are capable of, with what resources we can count on.

As the thinker Disraeli would say: "There is no better teaching than adversity". That day I had great insight into what it means to grow, evolve, mature and not age.

*The first step to growing and not aging is:
stop being grouchy.*

Often, a person is 20 years old and looks like he is 80 years old; others are 80 and look like they are 20. The secret is in the mood. A good-mood person has a habit of facing the world with hope, knows how to see the good side in things, always expects the best and not the worst, always looks younger.

Not only for the mood itself, but also for everything that it provides: good relationships, extensive circle of friends, ease in making friends. Grouchiness, on the contrary, generates in the person the tendency to always complain about things and condemn everything and everyone, that is, it is the anteroom of intolerance.

Grouchy people guide their lives for this feeling, end up becoming cruel and intolerant, especially with whom they love and for whom they are loved.

Once, I was teaching Master Mind at Votorantim, and the engineering manager, Adys Carlos Alves, said: "Outside the house we even managed to be relaxed, inside the house we end up being very grouchy". And it's true! Those who we love the most are the ones we lose patience more easily.

At another time, I participated in a political campaign as an articulator and among the activities was taking actress Dercy Gonçalves, a woman over 90 years old, to speak to elderly groups on behalf of our candidate. After the activity, I asked her the secret of longevity, of staying active, traveling around the country doing political shows and rallies and she replied that, "the best way for you to stay young is to enjoy life, see the funny side of life".

## 5. Business

Have you noticed how grouchy people take this grouchiness with them everywhere, having it as an inseparable companion, even in their professional activity?

*Language creates a posture, and
posture produces a result!*

What we say ends up reflecting on our posture, including the physical posture, and this is reflected in the result of the human being. Its tuning fork emits negative vibrations, creating a counterproductive environment for the favorable solution of any type of negotiation in which it is involved. If you need to burn gasoline to light the lamp, to ignite intolerance, grouchiness, anger, it is necessary to "burn" health. Is this an investment you want to make?

A friend of mine, Mr. Nilton Souza, from São João Batista, in the footwear valley of Santa Catarina, says: "Friendship makes the sale and makes life better".

Grouchy people have trouble establishing sympathy, affinity, rapport, plugging in, creating empathy with the other people. Therefore, they have trouble making sales, doing business.

The question you should probably be asking yourself is: how to avoid being grouchy? Each principle presented here proposes to cooperate with this proposal.

## 6. Stop trying to model others

When I was a child, we were in the kitchen of my house, in the middle of winter in western Santa Catarina. It was very cold and there, next to the wood stove, I started talking badly, complaining about two of my brothers - because so-and-so is this, because so-and-so is that. My mother looked at me and said: "Jamil, look at your hand". I looked at my hand.

She said: "Now look at your palm and your fingers". I did.

And she asked, "How many fingers alike are there in your hand?" I said: "None".

And she added: "So, my son, not even in your own hand are your fingers alike, and you want your brothers to be like you?"

The message was given: each has its own way, each has its own style, each has its moment.

By that simple example, which has been throughout my life, I guide my principles within the business world. When we are going to negotiate with someone, live with someone, when we have a relationship with someone, we need to understand that the other person is not us. And we are not the other person. Let's stop trying to make clones; stop wanting our children, our wife, our brothers, our friends to be like us, that our boss acts like us, that that client does this, and that, because if I were in his place I would do this way or that way.

Relax! Accept people as they are. Accept people in their way. By reasoning and acting in this way, it is much easier for you to win people over to your way of thinking, to make people like being closer to you more. It is a good alternative to develop and work on a pleasant personality and also a tip for overcoming grouchiness. Stop making mistakes, deluding yourself, because trying to model others is a terrible mistake, and that is not possible. Our boss, our client, the market, we are not the ones who model them. We get adjusted to them. It is an exercise in tolerance.

*The secret to living in peace with all is the art of understanding each one according to their individuality. (Federico Luis Jahn)*

These are patterns of behavior, of personality, as Richard Rohr and Andréas Ebert very well define in their book The Faces of the Soul. Learn about each profile and get the best out of each one. Offer birdseed for the bird and steak for the lion and not the other way around. There are people who have a geometric profile, the organization is straight, others are dependent on immediate recognition, others are focused on results, others are romantic, other questioners, other dreamers, others are harsher, and others preserve themselves for taking no risks.

These are patterns known as the Enneagram. The Enneagram is a deep system that describes nine patterns of behavior and their different levels of consciousness, thus helping people to evolve personally and professionally. Its origin dates back to the times of the Greek philosopher Pythagoras. It was brought to the west by the Armenian philosopher George Gurdjieff, in the early 20th century. It helps the person to understand why we are the way we are.

## What does this have to do with your desire to be a master in the art of dealing with people?

People are motivated only by their values, their profound truths. Find out what motivates each one, discovering their values. It is not for us to try to change others just because they are different from us. We need to understand the groups in which we participate. We need to admit the existence of different ways of being. Legend has it that, in the art of making friends, we must adjust ourselves to local customs, that is, "in Rome like the Romans. There is another Chinese proverb that says:

> *Above all things there are three points of view:*
> *yours, mine and the correct one.*

What does that mean? That no one is the absolute owner of the truth. So, please don't wish to be the owner. The capacity of adaptation means that the professional has greater added value in the market.

## 7. Control the criticism

If you want to build long-lasting relationships, control criticism: stop being the famous "whiner". Criticism is an instrument, a psychological principle of defense, that is, the person closes himself in a dome and criticizes everyone. It is a weapon fired by someone protected by armor. Very critical people never feel guilty about anything, they are never bad, they are never wrong. It is always the others' fault. The others are always wrong.

These people usually place themselves on one side – their side. It is a one-sided way of looking at things.

They are people who have entrenched themselves after their ideas and stuck on them. And they think they are always right. In fact, these people are on the defensive behavior all the time: they attack as a defense, to hide their own weaknesses. Remember that motto:

> *When you think the cause of a problem is another problem, it's because the problem is in you.*

Rhandy Di Stéfano, eminent American thinker, says that

*the human mind has mental models and sees the world through those models. Since we are unable to know exactly what is going on in the other person's consciousness, we evaluate it according to our mental programming, almost as if we were a clone of the other person's mind.*

Here comes the 90/10 rule: 90% of the negative opinions that people have about you do not refer to you, but to themselves! Only 10% have to do with you! Think about it; 90% of all criticism, complaints, labels, negative opinions you receive are not about you! How can this happen?

It is based on the fact that we see others through our references. Even simpler is to say that we see others with our eyes. Conclusion: we only see what our eyes can see, we cannot see what the other's eyes see. That is, every time we criticize someone, in 90% of cases the problem is in ourselves.

Sai Baba, an Indian thinker, used to say: "People are our mirrors". What we see as good in others is what we have as good, what we see as bad in others is also what we have as bad. People reflect what we have within us.

When criticizing someone, stop and reflect, introspect. You may just be projecting your problems, your weaknesses onto others.

I was at a shopping mall in Ribeirão Preto one day, having lunch at the famous Pinguim with Marcelo, a commercial director of Base Química, and he said to me: "Jamil, I'm doing a study on criticism and you are really right, there is no constructive criticism".

Each time we say, "I will make a constructive criticism", the listener closes himself in a shell and everything that is said afterwards he does not receive anymore, does not record anymore. Marcelo adds: "I have experienced, in my meetings with my employees, to always say what is good, and then I point out the aspects to improve, that is, I explain how I would do it in these cases. I notice that I am being much more effective in my meetings; I have been much more effective in my results, controlling criticism. I also realized that criticism is a fierce weapon, a cruel way to hurt, to hurt others".

Realize that we, parents, when the child is bold, creative and innovative, we criticize them. When our children become "boo-boo", we spoil them, which is understandable. However, we have the possibility to create in our children a mental schedule that, being creative and bold, they will be penalized and that, with complaints, they will be well taken care of. This can lead them to be complaining adults, grouchy, which will induce them to have a posture of slumped shoulders, to see if they can get attention. All of these facts lead us to become the popular boring. And we, parents, are the ones who can build this without realizing it, through our criticisms.

*A critical person builds walls instead of bridges.*

With criticism, human connections are not positive, effective and constructive. So be careful, control the criticism. Follow the example of Antonio Ermírio de Moraes: "Find no defects, find solutions". Anyone knows how to complain. It is very easy to find defects, to be a slingshot. The difficult thing is to be better than those whom we are criticizing.

*Find no defects, find solutions.*

Not criticizing seems to be overly challenging, however controlling yourself is possible. Remember that even a rose has thorns and the thorn is part of the beauty of the flower.

It is very likely that you already knew all that I said, but, as Renato Russo, the Brazilian rocker who delighted generations with his Legião Urbana band said: "I know I sometimes use repeated words, but what are the words that are never said?".

Control the criticism!

## 8. Have a smile in your face

The film Le Nom de la Rose, based on the book by Umberto Eco, in which actor Sean Connery makes one of his memorable performances, tells a story that takes place in the Middle Ages, at the time of the Inquisition, in a monastery in which young novices were mysteriously dying. There were some coincidences in these deaths. They all died laughing a lot after being in the library. It turned out that they read the same forbidden book. Because it is an old book, the novice dipped the tip of his finger on his tongue to turn the leaf and the leaf contained a poison to prevent people from reading it.

When the inquisitor went to speak with the person responsible for this, he asked why sacrificing lives to protect a book, and what was its content. He replied that it was a book by Aristotle's comics, whose readers started to laugh a lot and that was dangerous. The inquisitor then asked, "Why is it dangerous?" He replied: "Because when a person laughs, he begins to be audacious and audacity makes one doubt things and even established truths."

This movie taught me that when you laugh, you are audacious and can take risk in big things, even breaking your shyness. I mentioned this movie because of the smile principle.

*The smile is the international language of good friends.*

The good-natured smile makes life better. Greek doctors of the past, when they started to study the human body, they realized that organs have moods. When all the organs are in good moods, health is good. That is, good mood is a sign of health and balance.

Recently, an executive magazine said that good-natured people convey self-confidence. A good smile is a sign of mental hygiene.

Then smile. Please, don't save smiles. In addition, a smile is a facial exercise that causes the brain to produce a substance called endorphin, an enzyme produced by the human mind that causes a feeling of well-being. Every time someone exercises any physical activity, their brain produces endorphins and they feel that good mood, that pleasant feeling in the body.

When you smile, you move, you activate 28 muscles in your face producing endorphins. Therefore, of all the movements we make, this is the most pleasant and pleasurable.

And the benefits of smiling don't end there. It is scientifically proven that these facial muscles are not the only beneficiaries, but the whole organism benefits from smiling: the cardiovascular system is activated, the blood is more oxygenated and freer of impurities, the internal organs increase their efficiency. Want more? Yes, as if it were not enough to raise the mood, smiling is good for the health of the organism, warding off diseases.

And no one is so poor that he cannot smile, nor so millionaire that he does not need a smile.

*The smile is profitable.*

By the way, I would like to mention a friend from Bahia, called Jacob Lauck, a great coffee grower who trades with the whole world. One time, I asked him if he had already learned to speak English by doing business regularly with the Americans, and he replied: "Look, Jamil, in English I can only laugh, and everyone understands me". In other words, the smile is the international language of good friends.

Of course, joy cannot become a clownery, nor sincerity a burden! The smile is effectively a registered trademark. We are talking about the smile in a pleasant way; the spontaneous, authentic, relaxed smile. There is a carioca [a person from Rio de Janeiro] thinker named Ivan Lojja, who wrote a very interesting book called Those who laughs earns more money.

In this book, he analyzes some personalities like Sílvio Santos and many others, who have an easier laugh. Research shows that those people who smile the most are able to have more results, including financial ones. Hence that phrase "ah, the rich laughs for nothing [a heavy purse makes a light heart]".

But does a rich man laughs for nothing because he is rich or is he rich because he laughs for nothing?

Morris Mandell, an eminent thinker, said: "Everyone in the world smiles in the same language."

With a smile, you will be well accepted anywhere in the world. Laughter establishes a bridge between people, where pleasant conversations flow. In short, the smile is actually something that makes a more pleasant personality.

Don't live so locked up inside yourself. The value of a smile costs nothing, but it creates a lot! It enriches recipients without impoverishing donors. If on a daily basis someone is so upset or angry that they can't smile, then leave yours. Because nobody needs a smile more than those people who don't know how to smile.

Smile and live happier!

## 9. Be cordial to people

Be more cordial when greeting people. True cordiality is a spontaneous quality and should never be forced, but it must also not be repressed. You know that person who passes you by in the corridors as if he doesn't even know you? Do not follow this example. Regardless of whether this behavior was due to inhibition or concerns, we all agreed that it would be much better to live in an environment where everyone was friendly to each other. People do things for two reasons: because they want to and because they have to do it. When you treat others with kindness, warmth, respect and especially politeness, it makes them want to help you. Being kind, you make the person feel important, which is one of the greatest needs of human beings.

Develop this ability to be friendly to others. Of course, we are talking about cordiality in the broad sense, in the positive aspect of the word, not in a mushy, sticky way. Without the excessive need to be accepted.

Being cordial means greeting people with a firm handshake, being diplomatic, looking into the eyes, smiling, calling the person by their name. I once attended a meeting with my son Jason, who was 15 at the time, at an institution that aims to prepare young people for adult life. Among the jobs they do, there is one that is called the seven virtues, and at a certain point they are concerned with the relationship.

The guidance given on this subject is that no man, woman, young or old will have a complete education if they do not develop the ability to be friendly to other people. Here is a virtue that must be observed.

A professional who knows how to be friendly manages to relate better, sell better, manage better, administer better. As a consequence, he manages to optimize his personal and professional life, that is, be someone more fulfilling, who presents more results, with broader horizons and greater reach.

People say, "Ah! But if I am very pleasant it can make me look affected, maybe cause a bad impression, an idea of superficiality, of licking people's boots."

Roberto Montagnana, a journalist from Ribeirão Preto, told me once: No one is to blame if I'm in trouble - at home or at the company - and I take it out on elsewhere. This is a sign that the person does not know how to deal with internal quarrels, with inner misunderstandings, let their inner storm show in their frown, in their voice, in their words and in their relationships.

Based on that, we will be cordial with people, as this way we will be providing more quality of life and better results in the business world. Cordiality is an empathy generator.

## 10. Pay attention to details

Listening is interpreting. Not only the words, the sounds, but also the signs; for this, it is important to make good use of our communication channels to control our talents and abilities. When we pay attention to details, we communicate better with people, which makes it easier for us to make friends and achieve better business results, we expand our knowledge and form our range of values.

It is very important that we pay attention to details both in relation to our family members and our friends. This is also true in the business world; not only record facts, but act according to them, whenever it is not possible to anticipate us, which is the most recommended, in any situation.

## Pay attention to the communication channels

In addition, by paying attention to details, it is possible to identify the communication channels of each person, that is, how they communicate better with the world. The communication channels are three: auditory, visual and kinesthetic.

When someone transmits a message to us, it is decoded by the mind and registered in the brain, following certain patterns, whose values are distributed through the three channels.

Although we always work with the three, there is one of them that we work with better, with more resourcefulness and success. It's called a preferred channel. On the other hand, we have one that we call tertiary, with which we have trouble in everyday treatment and do not deal with the same ease.

Visual is the person who has the most reception strength through the eyes.

The visual values beauty, art, organization and perfection. It is detail-oriented, meticulous and prefers to explain things through maps, drawings and graphs, he is creative, he speaks loudly and quickly. His main value is rushing, he is agile, he takes charge of all actions and he is usually "the owner of the truth", or he totally alienates himself. Mentalizes quickly and, as a result, finds it easy to find solutions.

For the visual, the expression "eyes to eyes" has a literal meaning and is very important; if you don't look him in the eye when talking, there's a high probability that he will lose trust in you. The possibility of identification is to pay attention to his words and the way he looks at you. Some people use the expressions "you see", "please see this", "listen", "look here", "look at me when I speak". These expressions help to identify a look. So, when talking to someone, try to tune in, empathy, that is, to tune your thoughts with the other person and make it easier to deal with them. Use expressions like: look, see.

## How to deal with a visual person?

If you identify any visual person with whom you have to live, remember, do not mess around, be objective. Do not over-detail matters. Go straight to the main point of the conversation. When speaking, avoid interrupting. Wait for the moment they make a pause, then speak. Do not consider impatience to be negative. Always show that you can resolve things quickly. Be quick and show security. If you are dealing with extreme visual people (more than 50%) be prepared to be even more direct and objective. Do not be offended by the extreme frankness they may demonstrate to you. It is usually not personal. It's their structural way of being.

**Auditory is the individual** who best captures the world through the ears.

The auditory person values the durability and quality of things. They are strategists and politicians. They speak in a medium tone, with less speed and a medium level of voice, think conclusively, are very rational, objective and have the gift of simplifying things, continually interrupting themselves to see if you understand.

Knowing this, always summarize what you have to say to an auditory person; speak less, be direct and concise, as they pay attention to what is said only until they reach their conclusion, after that they tend to get bored. When sitting down, they usually look for a position where they can rest their chin on the palm of their hand, it is likely that they will not face the speaker directly, preferring to turn their head slightly to the side, to better apply the ear to the conversation.

When speaking, the auditory person uses the expressions "hey, listen", "listen to what I'm saying", "hear what I'm saying", "I'll give you a heads up", "Aha"; it resembles noise, it is auditory. When you have a dialogue with these people, use expressions that connect you with them. For example: "Listen to what I'm saying", "hear", speak words that have a connection with hearing. The ability to connect with this biotype is much easier and the possibility of them coming to like you is very great. It's like it is said in the sale: if the customer likes you, they will like your product more easily.

## How to deal with an auditory person?

Try to present a written proposal, detail the subjects as much as you can. When auditory people are speaking (they prefer to listen), encourage them by asking them questions and be patient. Do not consider their silence to be negative. Allow time for them to think and avoid putting pressure on them for quick answers.

If you are dealing with extreme auditory people (more than 50%), be prepared to be even more patient and normal. They take a long time to decide. Their coldness is usually not personal, it is simply their structural way of relating to the world.

**Kinesthetic** people (from the Greek kinestesis, means sensation, emotion, movement) are those who have their main communication channel in the touch, contact, in the feeling.

The kinesthetic people, on the other hand, are already more good-natured, preferring personal comfort, they do not sit in the chair, they spread themselves over it, too much tidiness or the need to be at places where etiquette prevails, can bother them. Their highest values are sensation, action, sensitivity to touch, experimentation and gesticulation. They filter out emotional actions and sensations such as joy, sadness and movement. They need to feel things, release more emotions, be more sentimental, cry easily and feel the need for sensation and physical touch. Kinesthetic people enjoy being in full action, like to dance, play sports, move things, fixing, gardening etc. They are attached to the sensations of the environment such as cold, hot, airy, wide; also to the weight, dimension etc.

They usually have a slow breath, tend to speak in a low tone of voice, more slowly, pronouncing the words better. Pay special attention to smells. A firm handshake means personality and reliability.

The way to identify these types of people is to understand how they communicate. Usually, they like to touch the interlocutor, touch the arm, shoulder, hug and often kiss on the cheek when they are the opposite sex. The best way to connect with a kinesthetic person is to use expressions such as: "can you feel what I'm saying", "can you imagine living it", "can you experience this moment or this scene", "can you feel the breadth of what I'm saying". With that, the possibility of tuning in with that person is exponentially greater. In the art of dealing with people, this tool has a powerful value.

## How to deal with a kinesthetic person?

When they are speaking, complement their ideas and, if possible, punctuate their arguments with affection. Try to show attention and make the conversation personal.

Attention: do not consider their excess of intimacy as something negative, nor confuse their way with the fact that they are "spacious", or very informal. Human warmth is the strongest point of their personality.

The psycholinguistics studies this subject deeply and makes it clear that the best way to harmonize with someone is to discover their preferred channel and enter into rapport (affinity) with the person, through it.

To get in tune with another person, first listen, listen carefully, observe gestures, posture, voice, intonation, order of arguments and vocabulary. Remember: every human being owns and acts with the three channels, although they do it with only one at a time. In the beginning it can be tricky to identify each person's preferred channel, pay attention to details so that your leadership and influence will grow exponentially.

## Know yourself

The phrase made known by Socrates in ancient Greece, 400 years before Christ, has never been so current. Those who know themselves have greater personal control. Whoever dominates himself ends up dominating others. Find your preferred channel and it will be easier to identify other people's channels.

## Test of the preferred channel

The test that follows was created in a language that is easy to understand, so that you can find more easily the way to deal with each channel. The important thing is not to be this or that channel, you are not, you are, because you use all three channels, but to know which is preferred, which is intermediate, and which is tertiary.

After this test, you will no longer have the "impression" that it is this or that channel. You'll know your preferred channel.

Each group of three questions indicates your predisposition to one of them. Position yourself in front of the proposition that most appeals to you in each of the three questions in each group - using your "feeling" towards each of them - and define the one that makes you feel most comfortable.

Give a score of three to the one you most identify with; score two for the intermediate and score one for the one that is less pleasant. At the end, add the scores obtained in each column to find your preferred channel, the intermediate and the tertiary. As an expert in psycholinguistics, I assure you that it is one of the simplest and most effective tests out there to clearly know your preferred channel.

Legend:

A – auditory

V – visual

K – kinesthetic

| Nº | PROPOSITIONS | A | V | K |
|---|---|---|---|---|
| 1. | What bothers you most when you get to your home: | | | |
| | A) TV noise, or someone talking loudly. | | | |
| | V) See the living room disorganized, things out of place. | | | |
| | K) Dinner is not ready or knowing that there is a lack of water. | | | |

| Nº | PROPOSITIONS | A | V | K |
|---|---|---|---|---|
| 2. | What is your usual way of enjoying your free time: | | | |
| | A) Listening to music. | | | |
| | V) Reading or watching TV (movies, cinema or video) | | | |
| | K) Eating, sleeping or acting dynamically (dancing, walking or playing sports) | | | |
| 3. | You learn more easily when: | | | |
| | A) You read aloud. | | | |
| | V) You read, summarizing or ticking what you think is important. | | | |
| | K) Writing or writing down things. | | | |
| 4. | When asking someone to do something to you, you tend to: | | | |
| | A) Speak objectively, only once, finding it absurd that he/she did not understand. | | | |
| | V) Speaking several times, or reporting in writing, to make sure your message is understood. | | | |
| | K) Speaking, sometimes lovingly, sometimes writing, or almost compulsorily leading the person to do. | | | |

| Nº | PROPOSITIONS | A | V | K |
|---|---|---|---|---|
| 5. | When submitting a written paper, you: | | | |
| | A) Write objectively what is necessary. | | | |
| | V) Write in detail trying to illustrate, with photos, graphics or drawings, because you think that appearance is very important. | | | |
| | K) You think that appearance is less important, and it is essential to show how much you "sweated" to do it. | | | |
| 6. | Your clothes are generally: | | | |
| | A) Classic style, plain colors, preferably in pastel and durable colors. | | | |
| | V) Colorful, always matching with the ornaments. | | | |
| | K) Loose and comfortable, above all. | | | |
| 7. | When buying shoes, it is a priority for you: | | | |
| | A) Price, quality and durability. | | | |
| | V) Beauty, they need to match with clothes. | | | |
| | K) To be light, soft and comfortable. | | | |
| 8. | You can memorize more easily: | | | |
| | A) Names, tone of voice, numbers and abstract concepts. | | | |
| | V) Physiognomy, shape, details. | | | |
| | K) A firm handshake. | | | |

| N° | PROPOSITIONS | A | V | K |
|---|---|---|---|---|
| 9. | You value most when meeting a person: | | | |
| | A) The tone of voice, the objectivity and firmness of their speech. | | | |
| | V) "Eyes to eyes". | | | |
| | K) Smell, taste, touch. | | | |
| 10. | On TV, your favorite shows are: | | | |
| | A) News, interviews and musicals. | | | |
| | V) Variety, movies. | | | |
| | K) Sports, humor programs. | | | |
| 11. | Faced with a new machine to make it work, you: | | | |
| | A) Prefer to be explained orally how it works. | | | |
| | V) Read the manual patiently. | | | |
| | K) Likes to press the buttons until you get it right. | | | |
| 12. | When you have to solve a business, you think first of all: | | | |
| | A) In the profit. | | | |
| | V) In planning or studying the details. | | | |
| | K) In doing, rolling up your sleeves. | | | |

| Nº | PROPOSITIONS | A | V | K |
|---|---|---|---|---|
| 13. | As proof of love, it is enough for you: | | | |
| | A) Hear the expression: "I love you". | | | |
| | V) Receive flowers and a card with the words "I love you". | | | |
| | K) A tight hug | | | |
| 14. | Your performance is best when you feel the need to: | | | |
| | A) Talk about the subject. | | | |
| | V) Write about the subject. | | | |
| | K) Doing something that depends on manual skills or building things. | | | |
| 15. | When an outfit gets old or goes out of style, you: | | | |
| | A) Throw it away without hesitating. | | | |
| | V) Keep it as a souvenir or wait for fashion to return. | | | |
| | K) Use it at home until it's wear and tear or start using it as a floor cloth. | | | |
| 16. | When watching a show, you observe above all: | | | |
| | A) Sound quality, acoustics. | | | |
| | V) Lighting and scenery. | | | |
| | K) The environment temperature. | | | |

| Nº | PROPOSITIONS | A | V | K |
|---|---|---|---|---|
| 17. | You can't get over something when: | | | |
| | A) Faced with a situation, someone does not reach the same conclusion as you. | | | |
| | V) Someone does not notice a crooked picture on the wall. | | | |
| | K) Someone doesn't cry or shiver at something exciting | | | |
| 18. | You admire in a person, first of all: | | | |
| | A) Intelligence. | | | |
| | V) Beauty. | | | |
| | K) Affection. | | | |
| 19. | You cannot understand: | | | |
| | A) Someone feeling hurt by something you said. | | | |
| | V) Someone who can live in a disorganized environment. | | | |
| | K) Someone that might not like a good massage. | | | |
| 20. | Do you think that a good entrepreneur should first of all: | | | |
| | A) Have a sense of profitability and practicality. | | | |
| | V) Keep the organization above all. | | | |
| | K) Act tirelessly, always be the first to get to work and the last to leave. | | | |

## Turn on your radar!

I have a friend in Florianópolis, Laércio Santos, who is very fond of martial arts and told me that in these fights, such as judo or karate, for example, it is very important to pay attention to the details of your opponent's movements to increase your chances to win.

You have to "guess" what the opponent's intention is and anticipate your moves.

He also told me that a tae kwon do fighter, to be a black belt, needs to know around 1,500 strokes with his legs, each one with a higher degree of difficulty than the other. But there are always some used so often that they become specialists, and that, therefore, these strikes are simpler to apply. When you learn something more complex, simple things become even simpler. For example, when we learn the multiplication table of three, we consider simpler the multiplication table of two; learning the multiplication table of four, we find the multiplication table of three simpler and that of two even simpler. This happens in human relationships. The more we practice this skill, the more positive our brain becomes, and it increases our self-confidence. Relationship and self-confidence help to dominate our fears, and the person who dominates their fears can triumph. The valuable message is the importance of paying attention to details, in any situation. Be attentive to the minimum signals given by our interlocutor, listen carefully. Both success and defeat live in the details. A company can experience great business success if it takes care of the details, or it can suffer a major breakdown if it is neglected. To have a pleasant personality, a manager, an executive, a person involved in business, must turn on the radio and pay attention to details. Doing so, will broaden the view of the entire relationship and make you a much more effective and productive person.

## 11. Talk about what matters to the other person and listen carefully

Those who speak well in public become admired. **Those who know how to listen, become loved.** That is why we affectionately call the Master Mind Lince course a "listening" course, which is a mixture of listening and speaking skills. Sometimes we say that we lost the audience. This is because people are interested in themselves 80% of the time. The one who is a leader has to have this perception and, knowing this, talk about what interests these people. Interesting people talk about what matters to the other, about what is important to them and holds their attention. The mediocre speak of the life of others, the futile, the boring, speak of themselves.

A known joke is that in which a seducer, with an imported car, a typical playboy, goes out with a girl, and talks about himself the whole time and at a certain moment - the girl already bored and totally uninterested - looks at her and says: "I'm already tired of talking about myself, now you tell me a little about me". Extreme example of vanity burning at 300 degrees Fahrenheit. Be skillful!

God, in His infinite wisdom, by giving us two ears and one mouth, showed that He probably wanted us to listen more and speak less. Apart from that, the human being's mouth can open and close, and the ear is always open.

Suggestive tip from nature.

## Fundamentals for sustaining a conversation

Show your interest by asking questions, ask the name of the other person, where they live, about their work, family, if they like to travel, if they have a hobby. Support the conversation. Try to know their opinion about a certain subject, about their goals, their plans and what is their outlook on life. In short, get the other person to speak and be a good listener, keep the conversation alive, interesting. Make an effort to know about their achievements, their accomplishments and, especially when you have an advanced conversation, ask for information about their social responsibility, what the person has done for their community, their street, their neighborhood, for their city.

Support the conversation, based on this motto: talk about what interests the other person and be a good listener.

One of the habits of the highly effective person is to listen skillfully.

To put this principle into practice, it is necessary to bear in mind, first of all, that the basic premise for this is to be willing to help the person. In doing so, in the end, we will benefit from building another friendship. Making friends!

Seneca, the Roman thinker, said: Don't ask what life can do for you, but what you can do for life.

John Kennedy, the great American politician, parodying Seneca's phrase, once said: Don't ask what your country can do for you, but what you can do for your country. Likewise, don't ask what people can do for you, but ask what you can do for them.

In the commercial area, it is very common for salespeople to lose sales by talking too much. What's worse: talking about things that don't arouse the interest of the other. In the 1990s, the focus was on the customer. The new focus on sales is to see from the customer's point of view. There is a very interesting parable about a couple who lived at odds, always fighting, arguing, because one did not want to listen to the other. They spoke at the same time and did not understand each other. Until one day the husband decided to seek the advice of an old and wise man, who handed the complainant husband a bottle of clear liquid with the recommendation that, the moment he entered the house, drink a good sip of this liquid and stay with it in his mouth, without swallowing, for 30 minutes.

He did this and, while the woman spoke, he was silent, desperate with the liquid in his mouth, unable to say anything. At the end of the 30 minutes, he swallowed the liquid and there was already the urge to answer the woman. And, so it was, for several days in a row, and the relationship between them was great. Asking the old man what that wonderful liquid he had received was, he replied: "Water! With just a sip of water, you managed to do something that is a stone in the shoes to many people: knowing how to listen to".

This is a simple story, but it contains a great teaching. It is up to each one to find his formula for learning to "hear the sound of the forest". Even if taking a sip of water.

*Listening is a transformative experience.*

Psychologist and professor from São Paulo Miguel Perosa says: "Listening is a transformative experience. It is to witness the existence". What he means by that is that, listening to others, we acquire self-knowledge, we know ourselves better.

I have a friend, Márcio Abbud, who is the general coordinator of ACEFRAN, responsible for the Universidade de

Franca, one of the largest and most reputable higher education institutions in Brazil.

I asked him how it is possible to develop a high performance management in an environment where knowledge is abundant, the intellectual level of the people who work in the organization is extremely high, in which researchers develop complex works in the most diverse fields of human knowledge.

And he answered me:

> *My secret is to work with people, to prepare them more and more for the group, and only through our attitudes this becomes possible. For that, we have to know how to ask appropriate questions, at the right time, and then be predisposed to listen to people with real interest, understand the feeling behind that speech and interact with them. In fact, I speak little, I prefer to listen more, because while I listen I collect important information for my leadership.*

Here is a beautiful example of what the ability to listen and speak can do for you. That is, obtaining information through attentive listening and with real interest leads us to the condition of leadership with smoothness. And it gives us space to get recognition, have access to higher positions.

Be skillful, be skilled and talk about what matters to the other person.

## 12. Do something different, something that adds value

In human history, everything possible has been done to control relationships, so that social interests are met. Families chose who their sons and daughters would marry. Rules were imposed to control who would be the accepted suitors. People of another race, culture, color, social class, religion, were not so considered. Nowadays, although less expressed, these rules still exist in society, like ghosts from the past that still surround the modern couple. Even couples who were not influenced by these rules and had the freedom to choose freely with whom to relate still deal with constant conflicts, caused by another ghost who is still trying to make one control over the other.

If control were a necessary factor for the success of relationships, we would not have the number of separations that exist today. An American comedian says that the number of marriages that fail is so high that, if the marriage were a commercial enterprise, no businessman would get involved with it. Of course not, because who would risk opening a business that has a bankruptcy rate of 50%? On the other hand, any sensible entrepreneur would learn as much as possible about a new line of business before venturing into that area. How many people do you know who have decided to learn about what makes relationships work before you have yours?

## In the past

Relationship success has never been a very addressed area, because it was not officially recognized that couples were unhappy, this is a modern event. Historically, this is even justified, since the majority of the population of the past centuries concentrated their energy on having something to eat, finding a place to shelter and having clothes to cover themselves. While people were concerned with these basic needs, the quality of their relationship was in the background, as subsistence required all their efforts. No doubt that marital infidelity already existed, but the right to want to have a better relationship is that it did not exist! A better relationship consisted only of having more food on the table, the rest was considered unnecessary, the rest was the privilege of the aristocracy. Social rules were created so that relationships were controlled. Man had his duties and was the king of the home, the woman had her duties and acted as his servant, expecting complete obedience from her. If she was not satisfied, it was her problem, as there was no place for her in the job market, so her only option was to keep quiet. Unfortunately, for the man, as he didn't have to satisfy her or to improve the quality of his relationship, he was not interested in learning much in this area.

## In the present

Currently, basic needs are met in some way by society. The dynamics of modern life provides conditions for seeking improvements in areas that have not been explored in the past. In other words, we want happiness in our relationships. Loneliness and a lack of quality human contact cause so much stress that they reduce the life expectancy of humans. Studies show that married people live longer than people who live alone. However, it is still common for many to complain of the wedding. But it is not that marriage is a failed institution, but that we lack the ability to create a good and lasting relationship.

> *The moment is different, there is a new world reality. To realize this, it is not necessary to travel the world, just look at the relationships between parents and children that you will notice how different the situations are. It requires a new posture. Sustaining a relationship is a task for people who put the law of success into practice to do more than agreed. Do something different that adds value. Transform the universe or just be another observer.*
> *A leader who is a leader does not conform to sameness: he is a transgressor of the conventional.*

He is the one who seeks a new order of things. It is up to us, therefore, to decide to belong to the group of those who make a difference or those who prefer to inhabit mediocrity, a commonplace for those who settle in the comfort zone.

Our future is the result of all our choices. If we prolong the timeline by repeating the same actions, we will arrive at a probable future, whose signs can be observed at the present moment of your life. We need to tell a new story, built gradually with conscious choices and an analytical sense. It is up to us to design the future we want.

The starting point is self-knowledge, through which one becomes aware of the established mental models and the limitations that seduce people to leave everything as it is.

The present is the opportunity to execute projects that create a new reality.

Ask yourself: what can I do more for my personal relationship? What can I do more in my professional activity? What can I improve in relations with my customers? How can I stand out, to be more productive, to have more recognition from my superiors and peers, in my work environment? Exceed expectations, surprise the customer, make him say: "Wow! This is more than I expected!".

Bernardinho, a volleyball coach from Brazil, says:

> *The will to train must be greater than the will to win, because the result only appears to those who are prepared.*

The difference is usually created after hours. These are the readings and discussions you do after the office lights go out. The invisible effort that no one cheers, as most cannot see. It is not simply the study, but also the preparation of knowledge, capable of adding skills and worldview.

Never forget that success is built little by little.
In human relations, it is like that too. Do something different.

## 13. Value the other person and do it sincerely

William James, the father of modern psychology, said the following: "The deepest principle in human nature is the urge to be appreciated". Recognize the value of people, know how to praise them. Do not spare praise, distribute it in a lavish and sincere way.

How is your ability to praise, to value people? When was the last time you praised your wife? Your husband? Your son?

Did you leave a note for someone connected to you? At breakfast, look at the person and give a compliment.

Highlighting the qualities of a customer, highlighting the virtues of an employee make these people feel important. But, of course, do it sincerely.

"Ah, but it may sound mushy."

What is it? There is nothing mushy about it, valuing a human being is valuing life, a gift that God gave us.

If you are asked what it takes to be someone with the ability to make friends, here are ten principles to quote in the first part of this personal development program. These are principles that are always dealt with in Master Mind - the leader with a master's mind - someone capable of making people feel important.

## 14. Summary of Part One

*You will learn,*

*After a while you will learn the subtle difference between reaching out and win a soul, and you will learn that loving does not mean supporting, and that company does not always mean security. You will begin to learn that kisses are not contracts, nor gifts are promises...*
*You will begin to accept your defeats with your head held high and your eyes determined, with the charm of a woman and not with the sadness of a boy and you will learn to build all your paths today, because tomorrow is uncertain for the projects, and the future usually surprises us.*

## THE ART OF DEALING WITH PEOPLE

*After a while you will learn that the sun does harm if you expose yourself to it too much.*

*You will even accept that people in good faith can hurt you sometime and that you will need to forgive them.*
*You will learn that speaking can relieve the pain of the soul.*
*You will find that it takes years and just a few seconds to destroy trust and that you can also do things that you will regret for the rest of your life.*

*You will learn that new friendships continue to grow despite distances and that it does not matter what you have, but who you have in life and that good friends are the family we allow ourselves to choose.*
*You will learn that we do not have to change friends, if we are willing to accept that friends change.*
*You will find that you often pay little attention to the people who matter most to you and that is why we should always tell those people that we love them because we will never be sure when we will see them the last time.*

*You will learn that the circumstances and the environment around us have an influence on us, but we are solely responsible for our actions.*

*You will begin to learn that we should not
compare ourselves with others, except when
we want to imitate them to improve.*

*You will find that it takes a long time to become
the person you want to be, and that time is short.
You will learn that it doesn't matter where
you are, but where you want to go.*

*You will learn that if you have no control over
your actions, they will control you and that being
flexible does not mean being weak or having no
personality, because no matter how delicate and
fragile the situation is, there are always two sides.*

*You will learn that heroes are the ones who did
what was necessary facing the consequences...
You will learn that patience takes a lot of practice.*

*You will find out that sometimes the person you
expect to turn his back on you in the fall may
be one of the few who will help you get up.*

*Maturity has more to do with what you have*

*learned from your experiences than with your years.*

*You will learn that there is much more of
your parents in you than you think.
You will learn that a child should never be told
that his dreams are silly, because few things are
so humiliating and it would be a tragedy that he
believed, because you will be taking away his hope.*

*You will learn that when you are angry
you have the right to feel it, but that does
not give you the right to be cruel.*

*You will discover that just because someone does
not love you the way you want, it does not mean
that he does not love you with all the strength
he can, because there are people who love us,
but who do not know how to demonstrate...*

*It is not always enough to be forgiven by someone,
sometimes you will have to forgive yourself.*

*You will learn that with the same severity
with which you judge, you will also be
judged and at some point sentenced.*

**JAMIL ALBUQUERQUE**

*You will learn that no matter how many pieces your heart broke, the world does not stop to rebuild it.*

*You will learn that it is up to you to grow your own garden and decorate your soul, instead of waiting for someone to bring you flowers.*

**Jorge Luis Borges**

PART II

# HOW TO INFLUENCE PEOPLE

For decades, I have devoted most of my time to the study of leadership. Most of this study is the observation of leaders in all regions of Brazil, through the Master Mind Lince course, because we are present with representatives in more than 20 Brazilian states. Everyone agrees that leaders are not born ready. Nothing in nature is born ready. We magnify throughout life. Leadership is a lifelong learning, especially adult learning. To lead is to influence people. The first step in influencing people is to master the ego. Some people's ego is so big that they have to be either the bride at the wedding, or the dead at the wake. They think that other people exist only to serve them in one way or another. They are people consumed by themselves. People like that never think of spending time elevating others.

## 1. How?

La Fontaine, the man who created fables, used to say: "If you want to convince, you need to make people dream".

In other words, if you want to influence people, you need to make them imagine that they are doing something with a greater purpose than simple obligation. Influencing people is to achieve collaboration and cooperation. Cooperation goes beyond favor - which is a spontaneous kindness -, besides the obligation and the power of command. A father can compel a teenage son to do something, appeal to the "down the throat", as they say in slang, making use of the fatherland power. The manager and the boss can too. But collaboration goes further.

Military organization is an example of command power; it is based essentially on this premise of strong command, but at the same time, military leaders also realized the need to develop their legitimate leadership power, based more on authority than on power to obtain the cooperation of their commanded.

## Leader-to-leader conversation

Money can buy many things. You can buy the workforce, buy the physical presence, buy the other person's time, a number of other things can be bought. But money cannot buy enthusiasm, loyalty, fidelity, presence of mind, talent, dedication, love from a human being. These are attitudes that have to be achieved and this can only be achieved with skills, with competent communication, in a qualified and effective way.

## Influencing is the art of negotiating

You need to know how to negotiate in every way to be successful. When you invite your wife to go to the movies, you're negotiating with her; when you try to get your child to eat spinach, you are negotiating with him. Keep what you've learned out of your home. Small actions are the seeds of great results.

Things you've learned over time. In fact, time is the best of all masters. It is a pity that when the disciple is attaining wisdom, time is up. What we can do is to redeem time through these techniques.

In business, what the best companies are looking for are professionals who can influence through uniting with others, giving and receiving cooperation to complete tasks and the pursuit of organizational and personal goals. It moves from the concern with individual personal gain to a focus on mutual gain, to the concept of seeking results in which everyone wins, bringing benefits to the parties involved in the exchange and to the entire company.

Whenever we are in a situation where we need to influence people, we need to think about the win-win method. We start from the premise that highly effective people, who always act in a noble way, know and practice this concept of negotiation.

The Harvard Business School, which is one of the five largest universities on the planet, in its process of management for results teaches that, in any negotiation in which one wants to win the collaboration of the other person or the company, this win-win concept must be kept in mind. This is a view of continuity, that is, the view of the Master Mind, which sees things with a long reach, with an entrepreneurial view, in addition to a single negotiation.

If I win and the other one also wins, the result is satisfactory for both sides. When it doesn't, on the contrary, someone will be dissatisfied.

Let's see below the table that exemplifies the win-win method.

| I | OTHER | RESULT |
|---|---|---|
| WHEN I WIN | AND THE OTHER LOSES | I'M MANIPULATING |
| WHEN I LOSE | AND THE OTHER WINS | I PLAY THE FOOL |
| WHEN I LOSE | AND THE OTHER LOSES | THESE ARE THE STRESSFUL AND NERVOUS RELATIONSHIPS |
| WHEN I WIN | AND THE OTHER WINS | IT'S THE MASTER MIND WIN-WIN |

Will I win? Of course!!! But the other person will also win.

A negotiation does not have to be seen as a dispute, a war, in which someone wins, and the other party is inevitably defeated. In this case, the relationship is exhausting, unsatisfactory. For example: you are a politician and are seeking an elective office; what will the community gain if you are a city councilor, mayor or governor? If your child leaves the bed tidy, the room in order, you will win an organized house, and what will they earn?

They will gain a more pleasant place to live. When you do a deal, a sale, or sign a contract, your gain is on the sale of your product or service, on the profit, or on the commitment made by the other. And what does the other gain? Gain with the benefits that your product or service will provide you, with increased credibility, get the bonus, with credit even in the relationship.

### It is the method of double-entry bookkeeping

Since accounting exists, the double entry method is used, that is, for each credit there is always a debt. Human relations are no different. Whenever we do too much, we leave a gap somewhere. If we go to football a lot, we can, for example, be indebted to our wife. We then need to balance our accounting and go with her to the mall, for example, or another place of her preference, which may not be ours. It is the same with children. If we work hard, we need to balance in another way, give quality to the relationship and invest time also in matters of your preference.

I have a couple of friends who are politicians in western Bahia. He, Oziel de Oliveira, was a mayor for two consecutive terms of office of Luis Eduardo Magalhães and Federal Deputy, she, Jusmari de Oliveira, a State Deputy for three terms, one federal and mayor of the largest city in the west of Bahia, Barreiras. Once, at lunch, I asked what the secret of such a successful career was, since she had also been a city councilor for three terms.

Each gave their own version. But the synthesis was one.

What do people expect from a politician? Return! In other words, I cast my vote and you repay me with something for my community. This is the double-entry, win-win method.

I was told that they guide their attitudes, always based on action and reaction, the double-entry method, because they know that what they say or do will have a positive or negative consequence. For that, they have three pillars of action that are:

① — Fidelity of the word with the action, that is, the word has value, the committed word must be fulfilled.
② — Respect for the partner - whoever helped them to come to power must be heard.
③ — Commitment to God - for the dream to be real, you need to make the flight plan and agree with the space owner, who is God, for things to happen satisfactorily.

It returns to the thesis that to grow, it is necessary to know how to compose.

In this case, with the Owner of the Universe!

## The fitting technique.
## Your win-win strategy.

In her book *Influence - you are also capable, and you may not know it*, Elaina Zuker explains what she means by this fit theory within this win-win mechanism.

According to her, influence is a positive process. You get the results you want while allowing others to also get the results they want. It is a mutually beneficial relationship. Your needs and results fit the other person's needs and results. This fit allows you to maintain your own personal integrity, while respecting the integrity of the other person.

While you cannot set goals for others that are only up to them, you can help them get where they want while you are getting what you want. Fitting is a smart way to ensure your own success. And it is the key to understanding positive influence. Other people become your allies and not your saboteurs.

## 2. The power in the art of influencing

However, for you to be able to play that role with greater ease, it is essential to have knowledge, mastery and awareness of the true meaning of power.

There is no leadership without the presence of a power that legitimizes it, that gives it validity. Let it confer authority. In every relationship, between two or more people, each has different sources of "power" over the others involved in the relationship. Being aware of how much "power" you have in a relationship at any given time can be of great importance. Likewise, being aware of the power of the other person (s) is equally important.

"Power" can derive from several sources. Some examples of these sources are:

**Specialization** — It is the power derived from the person's specialization, his knowledge and his technical capacity.

**Experience** — The power derived from the person's experience so far.

**Status** — Because he is on the "top" in the hierarchy, the person can "order" you to do something. The power of command.

**Charisma** — The power of the person derives from the strength of his personality.

**Relationship** — The person has power by his relationship with someone who is an expert, the boss, or someone with high status.

**Fear** — The person frightens others with physical aggression or personal threats.

What do you consider to be your sources of power?

① Think about the most important people around you, at work: what are their sources of power?

② In relation to each of these people, how do you try to influence each other?

③ Complete your power network in the drawing:

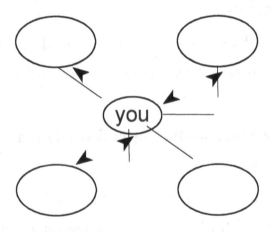

This tool will help you clarify what sources of power are available to you and think about how to use them to influence people in your relationships.

## 3. Be diplomatic

Often, when I was a little boy, my father, when referring to an intelligent person, who had feeling, who knew how to deal with others, who had social "skills", said: "That is a graduate man". This graduate term means someone who trained, who prepared himself, who built knowledge and transformed it into skills and attitudes.

Diplomacy is the antithesis of war. A diplomat is one who has distinct manners. The blow is firm, but with elegance. So, it is only exercised by superior people. People who has a title. That comes from the nobility. The commoner version of the nobility is the title. Hence the origin of the word diploma, a document that conferred the title. Previously, titleholder was only exercised by those who had title. The dictionary defines the diplomat as a person skilled in dealing with other people and the diplomatic as one who is courteous, fine, discreet. On the other hand, the diploma is something that confers recognition, a power. The Diploma serves to illustrate the figure of the Diplomat.

*Be a diplomat.*

The diplomatic aspect is built through relationships with people. This is a fundamental point of the economic operator: knowing how to win people to achieve what they have, and which is in their interest.

Diplomacy is the superior art and underpins the biggest governments. Peoples make wars, but in the end, they win those nations that have more intelligent diplomacy.

The best diplomacy in the world was that of the Roman Empire. It dominated the world for 600 years as a military force and in parallel, implanted a spiritual arm with the Vatican, however, for over 1,200 years. Its enduring for almost 2,000 years is not a reference to the greatness of the Religion it defends, but rather by a specific intelligence strategy in the art of diplomacy on the part of succeeding popes, cardinals and bishops who knew very well how to work the human psychology.

How to study and learn this strategy in the business world? Developing adaptability. Their multipliers are always local agents (priests), who speak the local language. The biggest political chief of Bahia usually says: "Do you want to be strong politically in the country? Be strong in the church parish". Remember this: You want to be strong in business, be strong with people close by. They provide support.

Any operator, manager, businessman and especially the leader, as a first gift, after his maturity, must have the ability to know how to produce functional people in his bunker. You must build them, because they are not ready. It is a problem that each leader must solve alone.

And what does it mean to be a diplomat?

What does it mean to be a diplomat in practice, in daily life? It is having elegance in behavior. It is the person who can apply the first principles presented in this self-development book in a natural way.

Diplomacy has achieved much more than war. In the Hundred Years' War, between England and France, for example, a river of blood was spilled. Diplomats managed to stop a century of bloodshed in two years, that is, diplomacy has much more advantage than war.

And what is it to be elegant?

Claudio Bolonhesi, administrator of São José do Rio Preto, said, at a leaders' seminar in Votuporanga that, if you want to influence people, you must equip yourself with the firm conviction that there is a diplomat in you.

According to him, being elegant is having a different way of behaving, which expresses kindness, gentleness, courtesy, correction. There is something difficult to be taught - and perhaps that is why it is increasingly rare - which is elegance above all.

We are not talking about elegance in dress, designer clothing, but elegance in behavior. It goes far beyond the correct use of cutlery, and it covers much more than saying a simple thank you. Elegance is that thing that accompanies us from the first hour of the morning until bedtime, which manifests itself in the most prosaic situations, when there is no party, far from the eyes of society. It is that unencumbered elegance.

This is possible for you to detect in people who praise more than they criticize, in those who listen more than they speak and when they speak they pass away from the gossip, from the little evils amplified in word of mouth. You can see this elegance in people who do not use a superior tone of voice when addressing a subordinate, the waiter, the gas station attendant, in people who avoid even embarrassing matters, because they take no pleasure in humiliating anyone. In other words, to be a diplomat is to be elegant, a gentleman, to be a punctual person.

This needs to be carved, it needs to be cultivated, it needs to be built with the patience of a goldsmith, who gradually develops a jewel that can become rare.

Diplomacy, nobility are virtues that can be acquired and sustained with skill and self-construction. Be the artisan of your performance. Leaders who prepare are more lasting, have more longevity in leadership.

## 4. Start in a friendly way

Laura Abbud, a consultant from Franca, uses this tool as few in the art of selling. See what she instructs us in this art of influencing people: "Whenever you are looking for someone to collaborate, you want someone to cooperate, you need someone - even in situations where you can just order - remember to start in a friendly way. In addition to making friends, it generates profit". Another field of leadership in which the dexterity of influencing people is often seen to emerge is the political. There are some politicians who have an extraordinary ability to sell their ideas, always starting in a friendly manner. Why? - Because political activity is an exercise in the quality of obtaining a majority, it is not the art of 100%.

The closing of this principle is: the habit of starting amicably opens the door to the request that is going to be made, or the collaboration that you want.

## 5. Learn to ask questions

Do yourself a favor: ask, ask, ask... When you ask, you organize and arrange the other person, you make them build bridges to the future. Who asks is the one who controls. Whoever answers are committed. Ask what the other thinks, feels, needs. Don't try to guess or, worse, think you know. "Guesswork" is the antithesis of good relationships, both commercial, business and personal.

I thought you wouldn't mind...

I thought you liked it...

I thought you wanted this...

I thought we were alike... and now...

The only way to avoid these constraints and be more effective and efficient is to ask.

In the art of selling, questions represent a subtle search, in regard of discovering the customer's needs, and then offering the benefit of your product or service. In the art of dealing with people, questions help to find out where the person is going, what the meaning of their thinking is, what the direction of their front is. Ask questions instead of giving direct orders.

Valmor Figueiredo, Master Mind instructor, always tells me that selling, for him, is asking questions and knowing how to listen, as he identifies the dominant reason for the purchase by asking questions.

Cristina Leva, a consultant from São José do Rio Preto, São Paulo, shared with me that she has already reversed several situations in sales by asking questions that lead to the solution. She told me that this tool has been of use without measure.

## 6. Techniques for asking questions

Why questions are so important to a skilled influencer?

Questions drive a discussion, attract attention and interest. Reveal how people feel about a topic.

They lead to development and interaction. They reveal the necessary information.

Check understanding.

They raise different points of view.

They lead to the solution.

Motivate action.

The skilled influencer sees himself as an investigator, researcher and explorer. He researches topics, values information and does not believe he has the answers. He looks at people and what they can offer the best. Questions are key elements.

Tips for asking powerful questions:

①— Plan your questions.
②— Be ready.
③— Use keywords for opening and closing questions. Ask: Who, where, when, how, how much, why, what happened?
④— Ask for specific examples. Enrich the discussion.
⑤— Encourage people to answer questions by asking them intelligently. Value the different points of view.
⑥— Show appreciation to people for their answers. Say thanks. Make comments when needed.
⑦— Avoid giving your opinions and ideas. Keep your role of coach, conductor, only play the role of mentor if asked.

I once came from São Paulo on the plane with Sidney Franco da Rocha, former president of Vasp and who had just win his second election for mayor of Franca, 20 years after his first election. I asked him what he attributed his victory to after such a long time. He replied that it was the ability to ask questions. For him, who was always an executive, life in the legislature was boring, he tends to do things in his own way, a strong command, which ended up alienating parties and people.

After going through a period of renewal of knowledge, in which he worked on this new strategy of managing through questions, he realized that the path could be different. By raising the political picture of the city's living forces, and the electoral density of each party, he began by asking himself first: Why did he want to be mayor of the city again? What would the city gain from his election? What would people living in the city gain from the election of their political group? – He answered them all in writing. In meetings with political parties and political leaders, he always asked the same questions. According to him, this was the time when he had more tranquility to create alliances throughout his career and did not have to do any "down the throat" to compose the coalitions and win the election.

Here is an example of how questions can lead a leader to be chosen to govern thousands of people and manage a budget that exceeds $ 100 million annually. The tool you already know. Using it, is in your hands.

There are some people you have no power over, and that's where the big challenge comes in. An effective way for you to get the results you want is to direct the conversation the way you want it through questions.

You give the direction that interests you to a conversation, to a negotiation. The ability to ask questions qualifies a leader.

Instead of going for the jugular, 'shin-kicking', or groping in the dark, ask a question. Clear the environment! How can we improve the arrangement of the furniture in this room? How can we better serve our customer?

How can we continuously improve our quality?

How can we find more alternatives to increase our sales by 10%, 15%?

They are relevant questions, which can lead to the solution of problems, or simply to improve, to make better what is already good. After all, nothing is so good that it cannot be improved.

That is, you raise needs through questions.

In his book Questions That Solve, Andrew Finlayson states:

> *We know that, on many occasions, the right question can make all the difference when making decisions or obtaining information. Negotiate wages and benefits, for example. The advantages and good results will always be better for those who have mastered the art of asking intelligent and meaningful questions. Life is a series of questions, because questioning is part of the essence of the human condition. In a world where information is becoming increasingly important,*

> *the ability to question becomes a fundamental tool for collecting this precious product. Who doesn't know how to ask fundamental questions to make decisions about the company and about their career can put their future at risk.*

We must often question to find the right path, to define our action plan.

And for that, it will be essential to apply this instrument with skill - knowing how to ask questions.

The eminent philosopher Socrates already used this art of asking questions and generating ideas, which became known as "maieutic" or "birth of ideas", which is a process of "giving birth to ideas" through questions.

Follow Socrates' example and extract from the people the useful information necessary for the successful outcome of the negotiation in which you are involved, asking skillful, pertinent, and directed questions. Exercise this skill, improve that ability and reap the rewards!

## 7. Be sympathetic to the other person's ideas

The political legend says that General Stroessner managed to remain in power for 35 years as president of Paraguay, making constant use of his ability to be - or appear - sympathetic to other people's ideas. They say that, when he wanted to put a president in a state-owned company, for example, he brought together all the politicians linked to that state-owned company in order to choose its leader - in fact he already had in mind who he wanted to put in the position, but he did it seems that the idea was of other people's.

He asked a senator who was a good name, and the senator answered: Ramón. He asked another, who suggested: Juan. And he wrote it down and commented: "It's a good name, look how interesting it is", and wrote something. And so, it went on, with several names being suggested. After a while he got the name he wanted. "Wow, look, what an interesting name", he was sympathetic to the indication and approved, as if the idea had been someone else's. He did it very naturally and what was marked was that he seemed nice to the ideas of others. In fact, he left it as if it were someone else's idea. He managed to remain in power for 35 years. It should be noted that, in this case, we have the concomitant application of two principles: knowing how to ask questions and being sympathetic to other people's ideas.

Now transfer this to the business world, take this to your relationships, if you want to influence someone, you want cooperation from a collaborator, a customer, a superior, show sympathy, show interest in the ideas of others.

## THE ART OF DEALING WITH PEOPLE

> *Understand to be understood. Connect with people's interests, try to understand and accept them as they are. Ask and listen carefully. If you are friendly, people will also seek to understand you. Your greatest asset is not made up of material goods, but the quantity and quality of the relationships (networking) you have.*

Being sympathetic to other people's ideas may be that, among the several suggestions, there are some that are interesting, that can be used. Quality comes from quantity.

> *In the multitude of advises lies wisdom.*

The November 2004 Management magazine features an article about IBM, which is one of the highest-earning companies in the world - $ 90 billion annually -, with more than 300,000 employees, almost 20% of Brazil's GDP. Do you know what the secret is? The secret, the difference, according to Rogério Oliveira, who is one of the directors of IBM Brazil, are the people. Knowing how to accept tips, because everything can be improved. This is innovation!

The view of market intelligence today is that people make a difference, and that relationships are crucial. If you want to be a master in relationship, a master in negotiation, an excellent influencer of people, know how to be sympathetic to other people's ideas. Know how to listen to people and your vision is broadened to make decisions.

## 8. Understand and respect the opinion of others

*The world is big and has space for all people, for similar and different people.*

*Try to understand the attitudes and behaviors of others, putting yourself in their shoes. Listen not only with your ears, but also with your eyes and your heart.*

*Use the differences to your advantage. What seems defective in the other, may be what he has or does best. Remember that what is different in the other is exactly what you lack.*

*And, don't forget - you are in control of your life, so if you discover that you are in the wrong place, with the wrong people and at the wrong time, it is because you chose it that way.*

Everyone has their opinion, from the most culturally prepared to people with little intellectual training, and they like it to be respected. If you want someone to collaborate, you need to be aware of that awareness of respecting the opinion of others. If you approach a dog mother, however small, with a puppy in her mouth, and try get the puppy, the dog mother will move towards you, it will be aggressive because she wants to protect her young puppy. Her protective instinct will be activated. The tiny mother aims to protect her child. This is the natural tendency of people to protect what is theirs, including their ideas.

So, respect the opinion of others, never say that the person is wrong, because their opinion is like a dog mother, it is something that they conceived, it is their creation. You never know someone's reaction when they are upset, when they are attacked.

And when we rebut someone's opinion, it's as if we're attacking them. The reaction, the defense, is spontaneous. It can be immediate or not, and can be kept inside the person, in the form of resentment.

It is very difficult, if not impossible, to obtain collaboration, cooperation from a person in these conditions. It is the famous law of physics: every action corresponds to an equal and opposite reaction. So, if we want to be efficient in the process of influencing people, we need to develop this ability to be very careful with the opinion of others.

On one occasion, having dinner with José Antonio Cicote, an executive director of the Rodobens Consortium, one of the 50 largest business groups in the country, who has thousands of people under his command, as he is responsible for the South, North and Northeast regions of Brazil, he told me that he occasionally needs to manage internal conflicts and uses this tool to respect opinions a lot. He said:

> *When a person comes and tells me a problem with their version, in reality they care for the company, I take this into account until I hear the other version. Respecting the opinion of both parties, it is possible to make more serene and less passionate decisions. This, in addition to reducing the stress of the situation, allows me to get much more cooperation from people.*

## 9. Human Principles Connection

You can open the door of a safe using a crowbar, sledgehammer or even dynamite. Either way, you will end up opening that door, you will be able to break it down. But, let's face it, if you have the key or know the secret, you can open it much more easily. This is the purpose of the tools. It is as if we have several keys that could easily open all doors. A master key. Even invested with the power of leadership, the power of command, it is necessary to know how to respect the opinion of others, just as the subordinate must also learn to respect the opinion of his superior. It is a two-way road.

Nobody likes to be manipulated, everyone likes to receive stimuli, and it is very difficult to get the collaboration of people who are not stimulated, are not motivated.

## 10. Command with skill

> *The effective manager keeps a steady pulse and a soft heart. (Vicente Golfeto)*

Never try to be too nice. It is a mistake to try hard to get along with everyone, being pleasant or submissive all the time. Someone will take advantage of this sooner or later, and you can't avoid problems by pretending they don't exist. Don't give in just to avoid a fight when you know you're right. If you show yourself to be a manageable person, others will surely abuse your good will.

In fact, you can even earn the respect of employees by being ready to "pick" a good fight (as long as it's not personal) when it's worth fighting for your goals. Shakespeare summed this up very well in the advice that Polonius gives to his own son in Hamlet: "Flee from getting into a fight, but, once in it, make your opponent run away from you".

Like it or not, while working in a competitive company you will always be fighting, and sometimes this fight will take place between the departments of the company itself. If it is a fair fight, without low blows, it will be perfectly healthy. In the case of fights with your colleagues, try to resolve the differences between yourselves, instead of taking the case to a higher office.

Likewise, friendship with subordinates must not be allowed to hinder the maintenance of order. Employees need to know that they will be warned whenever there is a need. Not even the harshest reprimand causes resentment when it is reasonable, impartial and fair, especially if it is balanced by praise, gratitude and adequate remuneration. In extreme cases, there may be times when the employee's dismissal or transfer will seem the best solution, both for them and for the company. If you don't face problems firmly, you will be replaced by someone who will.

Everyone likes assertive people, nobody likes rude people. But always remember that people tend to respect people who keep their word, even if they are harsh, more than someone who is highly friendly but who has credibility problems.

This same situation can be encountered during a negotiation. You cannot give up any and all gain in a negotiation because otherwise it ends up becoming a lose-lose or a lose-win, you lose and the other wins, or both end up losing, when in fact what is wanted is that both parties obtain gains and not losses.

So, stay tuned! This principle comes into play here: have command with skill.

## 11. Communication

A very powerful tool for command is certainly communication, so much so that it is considered one of the essential skills for professional success. And in human relationships, its value is enhanced. Why is communication so important to command?

Because the vast majority of distortions in relationships, bad deals, losses, great disagreements, dramas, separations, pains that last for years, violence and even wars are the result of poor communication. They are the results of what has not been said, what has been said in half, what has been said without clarity, what has been said without tact, without way; of what was misunderstood, misinterpreted. Ineffective communication can lead to rudeness and that is not leadership, but only commands that generate dissatisfaction.

The development of communication skills is an example of the greatness of a leader. How do you think it is the communication of a millionaire, a successful person, a successful business owner, an accomplished person?

Do you think they are vague, confused? Effective command takes this road: effective communication.

Train, train, train this competence.

## 12. Power and authority

Power: the right to decide, act and command. It's strength! It comes from the position. It is the external authority. Authority: authorization to exercise legitimate power. Internal authority comes from the example. It is moral authority. Among the leadership roles is the way of acting, the attitude that the leader must know when to adopt - they need to distinguish when to be a teacher, when to be an instructor, athlete or salesman. At a time is the manager working, at another time, they are a parent.

Either way, whatever the situation, they need to know how to be the right commander at the right time. Effective leadership does not mean being an always democratic, or autocratic, or authoritarian, or biased leader.

## 13. Realize the situation

Take, for example, the figure of a mother. In some moments, she is benevolent with her son, giving him affection, welcoming him into her arms, being a leader who encourages, supports and encourages. But in others, when, for example, the child does not want to take medicine, she needs to be severe, scold, exercise authority, without being abrupt, without losing her softness.

I have seen it happen inside my house, maybe you have seen it inside yours too, and I remember my mother running her hand over her slipper and saying safely "listen, eat this". Not that she wanted to, that she took pleasure in doing this, but because she was responsible for the process of "delivering" the adult child prepared for life, like a little tree, cut here, cut there, pruned and set. As she said from time to time: "The chicken's steps do not hurt the chick!". With parents, as well as with the manager, it is also the same thing. Sometimes, to meet the person's need at that moment, it is necessary to say no and demonstrate command. The situation of those who have responsibility for other people is very delicate. According to Paulo Rocha, a great human relationship expert: "People are not offended by what you say, but by the way you speak". Our tip in this case is: choose the right words and use them in the proper intonation. I remember one time when Yuri Goldstein, a commercial manager for Latin America at Netafin (an Israeli company that operates in more than 100 countries), hired me to run a workshop during a meeting that took place in Ribeirão Preto, involving participants from all over Latin America, at the time of Agrishow, the second largest business fair in the world. He determined the following for his HR: "I want you to hire

Jamil, who is a business coach, because he knows how to tell off without offending. He gives a slap on the wrist with such skill that everyone feels they have to serve him". I was hired, not for my résumé, but for my ability to have command, uniting firmly with smoothness. With this, I want to stress: a person must be able to command intelligently, with strategy, with security, with self-confidence. To have command with skill.

## 14. Surprise the other people by praising them

> *The nice thing about this is to make others feel good, it is a privilege of the wise, who know how to appreciate and publicly emphasize the rare virtues we have. Wise managers and leaders are the ones who understand that small praise is the purest, simplest and cheapest form of motivation.*

It is a human tendency to repeat an action that has been awarded. This is a principle of psychology. Every act that has been rewarded, praised, is fixed in the person's memory as something pleasant and that is why it feels satisfaction in repeating it. This works as a stimulus.

One way to achieve this is through praise, recognition. Once, we were doing group work, and Alicia Bonini, one of

Unaerp's directors, commented that the manager who praises is ready to be promoted to director, but the one who doesn't have that attitude is in his way out the door.

Why do we praise so little, then?

Because we tend to reinforce, even for the purpose of correction, far more mistakes than children's successes.

With that they can grow up with the impression that they are only able to do wrong things. Others do good things, they don't! It is no wonder that there is so much need for everyone to improve their self-esteem!

The adult, the result of this education, tends to work with an exaggerated critical sense of themselves and fear that, deep down, they may not be able to do good things. At the same time, they also have the idea already incorporated that it is others who do good things and that, therefore, they are not an expert at noticing what they do good. Hence the importance of praising, as the vast majority of people do not have this habit.

Ronaldo Leite, a dentist from Franca, has achieved excellent results in relationships, applying this principle. In addition to practicing dentistry, he is a professor at the Universidade de Franca. He is currently pursuing his doctorate, and it was precisely in this course that he had the opportunity to put this principle into practice - knowing how to praise - and proved its effectiveness. Here is report:

*"There are five of us in our research group, and one of them was somewhat apathetic, even though he was an excellent and well-known professional. One day he came to teach a class about his research. I was a little afraid of what the impact would be like.*

*His teaching was excellent, in every way. After his exposition, I waited for a moment when we were alone and gave a very sincere compliment to his class. He smiled, thanked me and I noticed that his eyes shone with joy. From that moment on, he became more of a friend, increased his enthusiasm in our work a lot, is collaborating much more with our research and increased his freedom and joy in our coexistence".*

William James says that the greatest desire of the human being is to be recognized. The yearning is more than a will, it comes from the soul, it comes from the depth of being. William James goes even further - he says that the urge to be recognized is as strong as the need for human survival. As leaders, we need to develop this ability to praise, to meet people's desires.

I remember one fact, working with architecture together with one of the best teams of professionals from the State of Santa Catarina coast, when we were in charge of building a very large mansion in Balneário Camboriú, in the Villa Rica condominium. It was me, Samuel Quijano, Álvaro Zaim and

Joilson Albuquerque. Álvaro introduced me to the foreman saying: "One thing I like is working with Joaquim, because he is a person who loves what he does". I saw that construction worker's eyes shine. And that house - whose construction we monitor - has become one of the most beautiful mansions in the condominium.

I say this to demonstrate that the person does their best when they are praised.

## 15. Have an appreciation instinct

> *It is said of Leonardo da Vinci that, while he was still a student and before his genius began to shine, received a special inspiration in the following way: his old and famous master, due to his growing illnesses and age, he felt compelled to give up his job, and one day asked da Vinci to finish a canvas he had started. The young man was so reverent for his master's skill that he refused the task. The old artist, however, did not accept any excuse and persisted in his command, saying simply: "Do the best you can". Da Vinci finally took the brush in his hands and, kneeling before the easel, prayed: "It is for the sake of my beloved master that I beg for the skill and power for this endeavor". As he proceeded, his hand became firmer, his eyes*

*aroused the sleeping genius, he forgot himself and was filled with enthusiasm for his work.*

*When the painting was finished, the old master was carried into the studio to judge the result. His gaze fell on the triumph of art. Putting his arms around the young artist, he exclaimed: "My son, I will no longer paint". (Streams in the Desert, by Charles E. Cowman)*

This episode is highly revealing of what can be achieved from someone when they have confidence in their ability, when they feel their work is valued, recognized.

At a Management and Direction seminar at Leão Engeneria, one of the business forces in the region of Ribeirão Preto and Brazil, its president, Carlos Alberto Leão, opened the seminar saying: "Here, in this company, there are chairs to be occupied". In other words, it valued everyone, motivating them for growth.

As people of action, as people of results, we have to develop this ability to create situations in which we are able to value the person in order to achieve his collaboration.

Praise is all positive that I think about the person. It is an opinion, a feeling.

Appreciation is the recognition of what the person is, whether in the professional or personal sphere.

It is more common for you to value someone's achievements, skills and qualities within business, corporate concepts. Appreciation is a topic linked to recognition.

*Have an appreciation instinct.*

Say how important the person is in the structure - whether in a political structure or in a business structure -, because appreciation makes the team work better. The amalgam, the cement that unites teams is to know how to value. It is a very effective way of being able to keep a team together, cohesive and, therefore, it is an essential skill for anyone exercising any kind of leadership. The leader, in their managerial role, should avoid as much as possible discrediting others.

*There are great men who make everyone feel small.*
*But the real great man is one who makes everyone*
*feel great. (Gilbert Keith Chesterton, English writer)*

João Carlos Benvenutti, a professor at the Escola Superior de Propaganda e Marketing and one of the great men of creativity in Brazil, talks a lot about the human capital of organizations and usually says that it is better to have a good team with a mediocre system than a wonderful system with a mediocre team. And how do you build a team of champions? Valuing people, making them feel safe; everyone likes to be led by a serene and valued leader. Value the dreams of your employees, of the people who live with you.

Ricardo Corona, a businessman in the auto parts business, on an occasion when we were having a coffee, shared with me that the most effective way he found to value the dreams of his employees was through trivial attitudes, small things but, for them, they were important. For example, getting your friends together on a weekend, taking an interest in their small problems, in simple things that become great when valued.

And there is nothing better to giving a person a boost of spirit, to lift their spirits and thereby obtain their spontaneous cooperation and improve their performance than to make them notice that they are viewed favorably by their superior and that his work is recognized, is considered important.

Enhance and put into action your ability to value the other person and the gain is all yours.

## 16. Sell your ideas in a dramatized way

Salesman Ricardo Juliano, who took a sales course at our institute in the City of São José do Rio Preto, said he used perfect copies of $ 50 bills to capture the customer's attention.

I would say to them: "I want to show what the result is in a certain area of the company". And he tore the $ 50 bill in front of the customer. This is a dramatization of ideas and a very powerful tool. He was tearing up that $ 50 bill to show that the company was tearing up money if it didn't use the process or product it offered.

And it worked! Another participant, Álvaro Pantaleão, businessman from Valentim Gentil, SP, to create an impact, also always had dollar bills that he handed out folded when he met a customer. This bill has a stamped eagle and he, showing this figure, made an explanation about the eagle's eyes, explained the entire structure of the eagle, the history of the eagle, the history of American symbolism and concluded: "Look, I wish you had eagle eyes, eagle claws ... to fight for your dreams and see them come true ". This has always marked his presence, who is a successful professional, businessman and politician.

They are skills of dramatization in order to influence people. Role play is an interesting tool. But without exaggeration! Dramatizing is a way to get attention. And it's not that difficult to dramatize. What is a child doing when he cries, screams, kicks? You're trying to get attention. It's dramatizing! And nobody taught her that, it's instinctive, natural. And what happens when you can grab someone's attention? That someone assimilates more easily and more fully what you are trying to convey. It's another resource that you have in the essential skills of the art of influencing.

## 17. Know how to launch challenges with skill

The challenge is our energy. Each time we challenge ourselves, we are encouraged to overcome it. The leader must know how to challenge their team with tact.

The role of leadership is to make people feel safe, to have self-confidence in relation to goals, because at first, they are weakened by challenges. It is common for people to feel insecure about projects and undertakings that often imply professional risk.

At that time, it was up to the leader to eliminate this insecurity and instill firmness in the person so that he/she increases his/her chances of success and is up to the commitment assumed, the challenge accepted. Always think about it. When you launch a challenge, you propel the person. Creating a crisis situation because the person feels pressured to make an important decision is always a tense, stressful situation. When coming out of the crisis, the person feels strengthened. It has grown, evolved. Every crisis leads to a solution that pushes you forward and upwards. The great inventions of humanity were born out of critical circumstances. Had it not been for friction, perhaps the wheel would not have been invented.

Do not forget that, in order to face the crisis with possibilities of success, it is necessary that the person feels safe and able to face it and it is up to the person who launched the challenge to provide the person with these conditions. Whatever the situation, the leader must know how to drive skillfully. Praise and then challenge.

When you launch a challenge, transfer responsibility, you make a psychological contract with that person. Without physical force or coercion, make this agreement, this psychological treatment; establish a relationship of complicity, of reciprocal obligations. This is a power of influence. The challenge has this condition of generating commitment; brings the person to the company's vision, to their vision, to the vision of their objective.

At this point, dear reader, you must be thinking: "Wow, but will I remember all of this?" Do not worry, as you absorb these concepts and reflect on what you're reading, you'll be sending mental commands, which will be settling in your subconscious and then entering what we commonly call the autopilot of the mind. The mind starts to react according to the context, according to what you are reading. Take it as a challenge!

# The short long road: the more you prepare, the more you gain and the less you work

Knowing how to launch challenges with skill is the delegation process. The very act of challenging is usually followed by delegation of activity or power. And what is delegation?

To delegate is to share efforts to multiply results through people. People need to be continually challenged to face new situations, to accept new responsibilities, which have been delegated to them to optimize the performance of the groups and to grow themselves.

As Deputy Delfim Neto says: "Who knows how to delegate can be in many places at the same time".

## 18. If necessary, step back

The sea is below all rivers. Even the most insignificant stream is above sea level, yet it is the largest. If it were far above the level of the rivers, it would not be the sea, it would be the desert! And when the sea decides to be above the level, even if it is only a few centimeters, the damage is great, just remember the tsunamis.

Making an analogy, when you and I want to be above, or impose our ideas and wishes, the damage is great.

Why that? So that you remember this principle: if necessary, back off.

It is the same as if you are going on a long hike and find a stream without a bridge. To get over this stream, you may need to step back a little; step back to get an impulse, a jolt to jump. So, if necessary, back off. In human relations there are also situations in which it is necessary to know how to back off, in order to be able to move forward. In a negotiation, it is sometimes necessary to step back, or simply pause, to have time to think, to review the situation.

## Soften the impact

In a negotiation, when things get stuck, it doesn't go any further, perhaps the most recommended is to step back. It is a matter of strategy. Many negotiators, when they find objections, think that they are going to war, fail to soften the impact, the poison of trick questions, difficult questions.

During a negotiation process, we must be very clear about what we want and how we should act. We have to identify where the problem is, if it is in the other, if it is ours, or if there is no problem at all. In the face of an adverse condition, an attitude such as: "If anything goes adverse, I get up and leave" is unacceptable. This is childish. At that time, make a strategic step back.

To lash out at it? No way! To "bang your head against a brick wall" is ineffective, something of unskilled people, without resources. Identify the problem accurately and act intelligently. If necessary, step back.

The expected result based on the imposition of ideas cannot be achieved.

Sometimes the negotiation is not going well or is not going the way you originally wanted. So, it's better to step back, take a breath, soften the impact, thank the other person for the effort, for the attention, than getting frustrated and throwing all the work done so far, mistakenly appealing to the "down your throats", or to hammer out, or hit. Learn to say the right words, suitable for the occasion.

*We call this shock of absorbers or oxygenators.*
*They are transition phrases.*

For example: "I respect your honesty", "good question", these expressions disarm the person on the other side, make the person more receptive to everything you say next. This is a strategic step back. "I respect, I appreciate, I agree" are phrases that neutralize the differences between you and the other person and convey a sense of appreciation to those who are participating in the process. You are softening the process.

What complements these phrases is not as important as the phrase itself. You can say "I respect your honesty with me", "Thank you for your time", "I agree that we have something to solve", "look, your point of view is interesting". That is, it is necessary to know how to soften the impact. In doing so, you are making a strategic step back, you are buying time, you are reasoning.

"What a good opportunity", "your observation is smart" are also fantastic phrases that produce excellent results when you are dealing with people. Know how to soften, step back, to create a favorable situation and get an interesting result.

What we really want is to win people over to our way of thinking. Be a strategist. Look from a more comprehensive point of view; it is like being in a room, in an upper position, higher, as if you were on a stage, or on a mezzanine. You look from the above, you see it in perspective. This gives you a privileged, clearer, more expanded view of the subject itself. And this more expanded understanding of a given subject can be the difference between an average result and a highly rewarding one.

Enhancing your cleverness in steeping back when necessary will further qualify you in the art of influencing people and improving your interpersonal relationships. To conclude this principle: In the face of an unfavorable situation, act like a five-star general - know how to step back and look over the canyon to be able to achieve your goals, your results.

## 19. Be tolerant

Legend has it that Henry Ford once suffered a loss to an employee worth $ 60,000 (approximately $ 200,000 today). He was asked if he would fire the employee, he replied that he could not afford to risk losing another 60 thousand dollars with another professional, as this new professional could come to make the same mistake, while the current employee could in the future recover much more.

We have to be tolerant on people we live with in a big undertaking, with our children, with our spouse, with our friendships, with our employees and co-workers.

*The danger of intolerance: leaving you alone.*

Those who think to find ready, able, perfectly qualified people have a great chance of failure, because they are rarities, practically nonexistent; finding ready-made people is like looking for a "needle in a haystack".

For this very reason, large companies, well managed ones, have a consistent professional training plan and designate an entire department devoted to training their employees. This is an extremely important differential for companies. And many people still need to "learn to learn".

Every time I meet a person who gives the impression that they already know everything, with the mistaken feeling that they are already complete - which is a serious mistake - I usually paraphrase Christina Tavares, a librarian in the city of Marília: "If you think you are ready, try to walk on water".

## 20. A good example

Eight at night on a busy avenue. The couple is already late for dinner at the home of some friends. The address is new, as is the road, which she checked on the map before leaving. He drives the car. She guides him and asks him to take the next street on the left. He is sure it is on the right. They argue.

Realizing that, in addition to being late, they may be in bad mood, so she lets him decide. He turns right and realizes he was wrong. Still in trouble, he admits that he insisted on the wrong way, while turning back. She smiles and says it's okay to arrive a few minutes later. But he still wants to know.

"If you were so sure that I was taking the wrong way, you should have insisted a little more."

And she says: "Between being right and being happy, I prefer to be happy. We were on the verge of a fight. If I insisted more, we would have spoiled the night. And something I learned with an emphasis on my married life with you is that the best way to win an argument is to avoid it. Therefore, I tolerate your little transgressions, because you are much bigger than them".

This short story, entitled "Being happy or being right", by an unknown author, was told by a businesswoman during a lecture on simplicity in the world of work. We have here a real skill class in the art of human relationships. She used the scene to illustrate how much energy we expend just to demonstrate that we are right, regardless of whether we are right or not.

It is not a matter of abolishing reason and seeking happiness through the approval of the other at any cost. It also does not mean to stop expressing opinions. Such an attitude could lead to many injustices. It is about evaluating when reason really needs to argue and when it's just an unnecessary loss of energy, compromising our well-being. She gave a practical demonstration of the principle: if necessary, step back.

She knew how to step back at the right time, softened the impact of the disagreement that lay ahead. It clarified the situation. One of the noblest roles of leadership is knowing how to train people, and for that, it is imperative to be tolerant.

## 21. Remember: scolding is the tool of those unprepared

If you want to have power, learn to have power over yourself first.

It is very common to lose your temper when it comes to the education of our children. It is unfortunate when that happens. With co-workers, the consequence is making the environment bad, tense, unbearable at times; with subordinates, the least that can happen is the loss of authority.

One of the most evident needs is to know how to control yourself, to have self-control. Without this, the relationship with our fellow men is very difficult. To achieve self-control, it is necessary to have self-knowledge and inner peace.

An Indian thought says: "Peace comes from within yourself, do not look for it around you". Therefore, our recommendation is that you start by cultivating inner peace. Stay well with yourself!

Carlos Castañeda, in his book A Separate Reality, says the following: "Take care when you use the sword. If you put your hand on the sword in a lot of anger, the wounded could be you". This is another side of the issue, the other side of the coin. Be careful when you have to be tougher with someone, because you can hurt yourself, you can get hurt.

If you are about to blow up at someone or something, remember that:

> *Anger is the wind that extinguishes the candle of intelligence.*

It muddies thoughts, makes the person commit wrong actions and make wrong decisions. Anger is like a fire that destroys, that consumes. Whenever you blow up at, you tend to talk too much and close your ears, not listen to what others say. Remember: those who talk too much are heard less. Pay attention to that. Furthermore, when you blow up at people, you tend to say things that can offend, hurt and will make enemies, lose respect and weaken your leadership.

Self-control is really crucial for a leader.

## 22. Summary of the second part

- Develop diplomacy.
- Be nice and friendly.
- Ask smart questions.
- Learn to be sympathetic to other people's ideas.
- Respect and understand the ideas of others and have command with skill.

In this way, the environment becomes clean for compliments and for the appreciation of people.

Whenever necessary, use a role play as a tool for achievement and collaboration, launch challenges with tact and skill. Sometimes, when necessary, you know how to step back strategically.

Under no circumstances, hit the table. This shows unpreparedness.

PART III

# HOW TO DEAL WITH DIFFICULT PEOPLE AND MANAGE CONFLICTS

## 1. High-performance leadership

Changing negative attitudes in people, without leaving them feeling resentful, is certainly a skill of the high-performing leader. It is the highest ability to influence people. It is not a task for amateurs. It is for those who want to be big. Leaders are not defined by easy times, but by challenging times. Can you think of Barack Obama, for example, complaining that he can't do it? Dealing with these challenging personalities is certainly an opportunity to develop the leader in you. Legend has it that when we pray to God and ask for tolerance, He always puts a difficult person on our side. It is to strengthen the emotional muscles.

Leadership, in its breadth, involves a life project far beyond mediocrity.

Among the many challenges that imply being human, there is certainly the ability to deal with difficult people. In the great relationship building project, we come across often with some life situations that seem to be repetitive - patterns that are repeated and that sometimes lead us to exclaim: "phew! what a difficult person to relate to!".

How many people do you know who are bitter, who seem to complain all the time about their endeavors, about their life, even seem to attract bad things, culminating in most cases in a sequence of failures. It seems that they always live a series of tragic and destructive dramas in their lives. This negative pattern of life, which accompanies these people, ends up making them become undesirable types, of difficult interpersonal relationship.

You and I know how much easier life would be if we didn't have to deal with difficult people. Relationships would be harmonious and there would be more justice and tolerance in the world.

But isn't there anything we can do to eliminate some wear and tear when dealing with these people? Are there any secrets to making our relationships more harmonious and more effective even when difficult people come along the way?

We are talking about our daily life, about our daily personal interactions - family, work, business, friends, social life.

Some people are really very challenging! It seems that they have a pattern, they form types, and may even establish a classification of difficult personalities, by model, by type. And they guide their lives by these standards.

In this way, we can identify the aggressive types, those who are always attacking someone with words. They give the impression that they feel happy to attack, to provoke. They are hostile by their own, they are prickly, antagonistic. There is one who only knows how to complain - complains all the time, grumbles. They keep complaining about others and about life. It's the complainant type!

Another notorious type is closed or inhibited. They are the one who is always silent, they look like an oyster, impenetrable. To get some information from these people we say that it is necessary to "take it out with a corkscrew". It is very difficult to get him out of the cocoon and deep down they are a sensitive individual, they are not exposed, afraid of being rejected. They never have a subject, they do not speak to anyone, they are the type of person who ends up isolating themselves, they do not reveal their thoughts, their feelings.

They often end up characterizing themselves as a loner, they live alone and within their world, as they have great difficulty communicating with others. This attitude ends up affecting the whole group.

There is also the suspicious, the one who feels threatened all the time. It seems that everything bad that happens around them is the result of actions that have the purpose of harming them. They do not trust anyone, they are even suspicious of their own shadow. It is important, then, before we get angry, offend them, or even to despise them, that we try to understand what their problem is, what is afflicting them. Once you understand this - with the problem solved, or with your solution forwarded - you will certainly have a person willing to cooperate by your side.

One of the most serious cases of difficult people are addicts, which is the great human challenge of relationships - dealing with the negative attitudes of a person who has their addictions, their habits.

I have a friend, the psychologist Jéferson Fuza, who used to say: "Look, going for the jugular, 'shin-kicking', anyone can do it. Hard is to deal skillfully with these difficult people".

We often have to endure and live with these people. What usually happens is that we put up with it, until one day we can't take it anymore and we blow up. We start bad mouthing everything. The result is already known: pure stress.

Our proposal in this third module is to present some tools that can help to see others,

## 2. Focus on something good on the person first

*In every person, even if they are a thug, there is at least 5% kindness. (Baden Powell)*

*Hold a brief meeting to resolve the matter.*

The first step is: focus on something good on the other person first.

It is more or less like when a man shaves: before shaving, he always puts some shaving foam. First, the good part, the easier job. When you are going to deal with someone who has a difficult personality, the first recommendation is that, if you "play hard", confronting the person, you will create problems. Avoid being rude. Avoid confrontation. With skill, call the person, sit down with them, if applicable, and say: we need to talk.

If you are a leader, if you are a manager, if eventually you are a person who has influence, start the conversation by highlighting something positive and good about the other person, such as: "You are a person of potential", "You are a person that I respect, that I admire", "You are a person that I love ".

Michele Rissi de Castro, a psychologist from Franca, used to say:

> *First, create a tune, and then, drive.*
> *Before making the cake, you need*
> *to grease the cake tin.*
> *(Dona Flora)*

Soften, prepare the ground, do not create more problems, more stress. Use the "start friendly" principle. Start by softening the conversation, showing interest in finding solutions, not in creating problems. The idea is to lead the process towards resolving the deadlock or conflict, adopting a posture of a person of solution, of result, and not as someone who gets emotionally involved in the process and is in a neurotic, exhausting, fruitless relationship. In fact, this is the difference between the exciting person and the emotional person. The exciting person manages their emotion and manages to move others. They generate energy in the environment. The emotional person, in the face of situations that involve feelings, lets themselves be involved by them and is overwhelmed by emotion.

> Celebrate what went
> right and correct
> what went wrong.

When you emphasize the good aspects of the person, they end up, by comparison with their defects, concluding that it is not worth continuing (at least at that moment) to demonstrate these defects, or their points to improve. Their negative aspects are weakened by the strength of their qualities. It is as they say, in Barretos, São Paulo, "to have the horns of an angry bull cut off".

## 3. Avoid unnecessary discussions and problems

Never use bad language in situations where you have to deal with people who are difficult to deal with. You will do well to avoid common terms. Swearing can be offensive without you even realizing it.

In fact, vulgar and even obscene language is routinely used in certain circles. Sometimes it happens that this language is imported into the work environment due to the supposed "effect" it produces. There are those who believe that it is a sign of power or vigor. The problem is that only the listener knows what the real effect is, and he can reach a conclusion very different from that intended by the speaker. In any case, obscene language is not suitable for anyone and a "dirty mouth" does not usually arouse anything but contempt.

In addition to all considerations of an ethical and moral nature, there are very valid practical reasons for you to preserve the uprightness of your character.

If you keep your personal integrity high, you will be a trustworthy, responsible and sincere person. The reward for this type of attitude is trust - from your colleagues, subordinates and external contacts.

The personality of a person around you tends to become more transparent to you over time. A short period is enough for individuals to be recognized, analyzed and cataloged for what they are, with a much greater accuracy than they imagine. This makes anyone look ridiculous when he poses or tries to convince himself that he is someone different from what he really is. As Ralph Waldo Emerson said: "What you are resonates in such a way that I cannot hear what you say to the contrary". Therefore, it is up to you to let your personal conduct, both explicitly, represent the standard of personal and professional integrity by which you would like the world to esteem and classify you.

When you are in a stressful situation with someone, remember this principle:

Denise Alcântara and Paulo Pellizzon, Master Mind instructors from Orlândia, who told me about this principle at the time they were dealing with difficult people. They told me:

*The only way to win an argument is to avoid it. In a discussion, everyone loses. It is a "lose-lose" concept".*

You can be 99% right on a certain topic, but once you start arguing, that 1% can make you lose the discussion. Instead of one problem, you will have two.

The discussion is, in itself, an intractable situation, the person starts by accusing, pointing the finger, complaining, calling attention and a tense atmosphere is established at the beginning. The tuning fork is always out of place, that is, we have more problems to be solved right away. React with questions, never with offenses.

## 4. Ask questions that lead to the solution

One way to change a behavior, which is sometimes difficult, is certainly knowing how to ask questions. Maurício Amorim, one of our coordinators, reversed a conflict situation with a participant who presented a highly harsh behavior, asking him questions. The participant himself confessed that his behavior was a product of excessive pressure and that he was too stressed. Our programs are oriented so that people can manage their attitudes under pressure, overcome concerns and enjoy life more. That participant became a great champion of our training in that northeastern sector of via Anhanguera.

Pryscila Liboni, commercial manager at W&A in Franca, in one of her lectures on sales, warned about the importance of knowing how to influence people. She said that she once went to negotiate shoe soles with a client in Santiago, Chile. Initially, the attitude of her future customer was unfriendly, and the dialogue was becoming a monologue. According to him, his sole supplier supplied the needs of his company. However, she noticed that this client's wife, who was present at the meeting, often looked at her shoes. Pryscila remembered the yellow light of the traffic light - pay attention to the details. Gently and sympathetically, she praised (sincerely) the color of that lady's hair and the three began to talk. In an informal and friendly way and through her questions, she created the situation and took her as far as she wanted to get: shoes.

Her client's wife commented on her shoes, and she offered them for her to put them on. The woman praised the comfort and softness of the shoes. Pryscila then took the opportunity saying that the reason for being comfortable and light was in the sole. She got a first smile from her customer. With a few more minutes of conversation, she managed to affect the first order, of many others which would come. She realized that influencing people is easier when you create attunement at first, because if people like us, it is easier to accept our products and reverse difficult situations. Below is a graph representation of how to conduct appropriate questions.

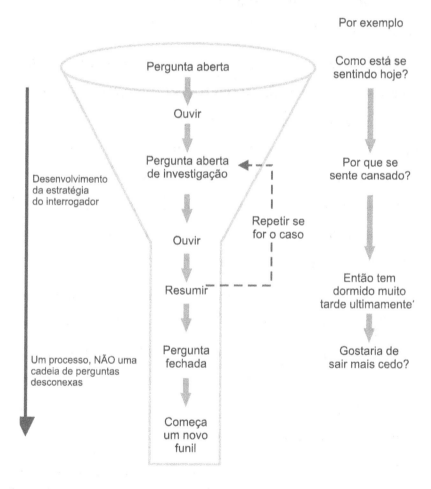

[Legend]: Development of interrogator strategy; A process, NOT a chain of disconnected questions; Open question; Listen; Investigation open questions; Listen; Summarize; Closed question; A new funnel starts; Repeat if applicable; For example; How are you feeling today? Why do you feel tired? So, have you going to be late night lately? Would you like to go out earlier?

## 5. Avoid sharply pointing errors

*Never embarrass the other person.*

I praise it out loud and blame it in a low voice, said Catharina of Russia.

Avoid the direct blow, which humiliates the other. Pointing out the error drastically is a very provocative, shocking action, which causes unease, even more when the person has internal conflicts. It is possible that, in doing so, you may hurt the other's self-esteem, committing an injustice or making the other feel wronged. Caution! You can destabilize or unbalance a person in the face of a situation in which you are trapped, challenged by aggressive, rude words.

You can be absolutely sure that nobody is difficult because they like to be difficult. You can be convinced that if you take an aggressive stance against someone, you will be confronted with hostility. It may be causing unexpected reactions, awakening problems that are often dormant. Using a slang, we can say that you will be "stirring up on a hornet's nest".

It seems obvious, doesn't it? But it is not. We can be easily surprised by appearances. That is, you will behave harshly and may have very unpleasant surprises. So, before you get angry at someone, because of a behavior that you thought was wrong or hostile, or inappropriate, or unfair, or even aggressive, think carefully before confronting the person, "pointing the finger". There is a saying that when you point your finger at another person, there are three fingers pointed at yourself and one at the sky. So, if you close your hand with your index finger forward, you will see that the tendency is to keep your thumb pointing upwards and the other three fingers pointing at you. So, if you don't want to take unnecessary risks, avoid pointing out mistakes in a harsh way, never embarrass the other person.

## 6. Allow the other person to try again

*Welcome, correct and support.*

First, start in a friendly way and say something good, positive, highlighting some aspect of the person - notice that we have in action here, at the same time, the principles "start friendly", "know how to praise" and "focus first on something good about the person".

Then, talk about what needs to be improved - it's the negative. Here comes the correction. "Look, you have potential, technical capacity, but I need you to do this, I need you to improve on this, on that."

One way to ease this phase is to point out that what is good can always be improved. Nothing is so good that it cannot be improved! Once again, we have the simultaneous application of principles already seen, which in this case are "have command with skill" and "know how to launch challenges".

And the third is again a positive - encouraging, is the support. It is an invitation to try again. "Look, I know you can; I trust you; you have potential; you are the person who can do the job; I believe that you can overcome this addiction; I'm sure you can achieve your goals; I know you made a mistake trying to do your best and next time you will get it right. "It is the phase of appreciation and challenge.

Dr. José Paulo Rodrigues, a physician and specialist in transactional psychoanalysis, in a lecture on transactional analysis, told us that an indicator of maturity is knowing how to accept adverse situations, deal with them and, mainly, encourage correction with skill. What is this if not the PNP in action? You have this tool at your fingertips. Use it.

Make a continuous effort in this direction, commit yourself to this, keep in mind that dealing with difficult people requires a great deal of compassion from human beings. We need to be concerned with human beings, with others. We need to get used to this idea of giving the person a chance to try again. This is an aspect of the human relationship that has to be worked on by everyone who intends to be successful in life. After all, life is a great gift from God that needs to be taken care of. We are going to take care of this divine gift, constantly improving our qualities, to live harmoniously with difficult people.

*Reinforcing the concept: welcome,*
*correct and support.*

## 7. Encourage, when progress is made

When someone tries again, praise the performance. It is a continuation, a complement to the previous principle - allow the other person to try again -, a crowning achievement of the plus-minus-plus process. Remember the "know how to praise" and "value the other person" principles. This is an appropriate time to apply them. Do not forget that everything that is praised is likely to be repeated. In that case, you are encouraging the person to repeat the feat of having accomplished something good and to make it a habit. It may be that she ends up not being a difficult person. This is a humanist proposal. Whatever your activity, dealing with people should be your primary function.

Amílcar Melendez is a chemical engineer and president of Avon Brasil. Asked what he would do if he were deciding his future today, he said so:

*I would study engineering again, because of logical reasoning. But I would choose a course with a heavy weight in humanities. To become president of a company, one must have a genuine interest in people, motivate them and make them grow. Uniting knowledgetechnical and humanistic traits is essential in any business activity.*

This supports everything I have been saying so far about the importance of human talent and the relationship between people in the business world in today's economy. In the teams: for sure, the best way to strengthen team spirit is to encourage, allowing the person to try again.

To highlight the importance of team activity, I would like to quote an excerpt from the book Acorde para o sucesso, by Guilherme Cirali:

> *No one else is a lonely navigator. Not even the modern hero of the seas, Amyr Klink, who, even physically alone, has a highly competent team during the trips, from the project's design to its effective implementation and monitoring.*

I think this memory of the figure of Amyr Klink, who has his brand in solitude, is very appropriate and, however, the success of his work is totally dependent on the work of a team. Actually, it is not a loner, but a team acting. A team in which individual defects do not override common goals. The difficult side of people disappears when they are stimulated, when they realize that their progress is being recognized, their performance is being praised.

Nothing better - to have a cohesive, vibrant, active team - than maintaining the motivation of its members by stimulating people, praising, extolling the performance of each one.

## 8. Admit that you also make mistakes

The raw material of experience is the error. Just as the raw material for character is the respect. Taking responsibility for your mistakes is one of the greatest manifestations of intelligence, character and maturity that can exist.

Nobody is perfect. In fact, perfect people must be pretty boring. Nobody likes hypocrites. In a relationship, if there is a possibility that you can talk to the person (we are talking about challenging people), a chance exists that there is an understanding is always the best way. The way of understanding is always the right road to take. When you admit that you also make mistakes, you humanize yourself, and by humanizing yourself, you allow the other person to face you differently too, because, strictly speaking, who likes scolds? When you assume that, from time to time, you made mistakes, you can rest easy, your authority is not shaken. In fact, it is growing a lot. Recognizing your own mistake is an exercise in humility and also honesty above all with yourself.

## 9. Remember the three "R's"

- Respect for others.
- Respect for yourself.
- Responsibility for your actions.

Respect for others, the first "R", is a commandment that Jesus taught us. Remember the Master of Masters, the Master of Sensitivity, when he said, "Love your neighbor as yourself".

Have this view that respecting others is fundamental. It's another humanist proposal that we're presenting within this great challenge that is to deal with the human factor as a determining factor in our relationships.

Take care not to attack, not to hit, not to offend, not to hurt, not to create riots, open wounds, which sometimes take long years or even a lifetime to be healed. Respect others. Everyone has their difficulties, their reasons; who knows what paths have been taken. What is certain is that it is not for us to judge anyone, but to respect their reasons.

The second "R" is self-respect. Have you noticed that sometimes, when a person is stressed, he loses respect for himself? And what happens when we are facing a difficult person? Generally, if it is difficult, you end up being affected internally. The contact with this type of person, by itself, generates some anxiety, creates difficulty. It is, by nature, a stressful contact. This ends up creating challenging situations and that is when the person happens to lose respect for himself. I remember an episode that happened to me at home. One day, I can't quite remember why, I ended up having a blow up - the kind that you curse, stomp your foot on, hit your hand with, and all those things we do when we have blow-ups. After the psychological burst phase, after that unpleasant sensation, I sat in the living room, thoughtful. After a while, my middle daughter, Jusanflora, who was nine or ten at the time, came up to me, sat across from me and said: "Dad, what a blooper you made, huh!". I looked her right in the eye and said, "Yeah, it happens."

Have you noticed that when we blow up and then stop to think, the conclusion is that we end up not respecting ourselves? That we make a blooper and that gives a damned moral hangover? There is nothing worse than a moral hangover. You know it.

*So, respect yourself.*

The third "R's" is the responsibility for your actions. Be careful, because the impact of attitudes can be very great, especially of blunt actions.

Once I was traveling to São Paulo, by plane, reading a newspaper and there was a headline that read: "Architect kills owner of a construction company". That caught my attention. I usually do not read the police pages of newspapers, because I prefer to read the good news over tragedies. It is a personal decision. But that news caught my attention because architecture is an area that I like and I know that the profile of this professional is closely linked to sensitivity, and not to violence.

As I read the article, I realized that the architect had been offended. He was a resident architect (those professionals who go to the work when it is in the finishing phase; his work is integral within the work, following the entire process of finishing the construction - he does not provide occasional services). The entrepreneur, apparently, should be one of those harsh, blow up people, perhaps even a difficult person. That is what I concluded, although I did not know him and was not there to confirm it. But that was what it seemed to me. It was reported that he offended the architect in front of the construction workers and when he turned his back, the architect took a wood that was close to his hand and hit it on the businessman's back, which fell and with the blow ended up breaking his neck.

A tragedy. One lost his life, the other, his freedom.

That man who offended the architect was probably not a cruel person, he was certainly not a bandit, he was a person like you and me. A job generator, a fighter, a taxpayer, a good citizen, but maybe at his limit, in a stressful situation, he had a moment of explosion, he did not think about the responsibility of his actions and when he acted like that he ended up provoking a reaction that took his life. And the architect ended his entire life story.

Here is an example of what a thoughtless action, without measuring your responsibility, can bring. We need to keep the responsibility for our actions in mind, first of all.

If we analyze some family dramas, such as children who take their parents' lives or who lose their lives at the hands of their parents, we will see that behind these tragedies is the lack of respect for others, for themselves and irresponsible actions. It is the fruit of coexistence between difficult people and with no idea how to act in these circumstances.

Have no doubt that when you deal with difficult people, you are on the borderline - you are on the borderline, as they say in psychoanalysis. On the borderline, you can make a misstep and fall. It is as if he were walking on the edge of a mountain and, at the slightest carelessness, he might fall into the cliff. You're on the edge. So, when dealing with these people, be clear that you are on an edge and don't forget the responsibility for your actions. In doing so, the result will always be better, always more effective, and you will feel peace of mind. One of the greatest pursuits of the human being is inner peace. Acting according to the "3 R's" you will always have inner peace.

## 10. Give a person a good reputation

The profession of a football coach is undoubtedly one of the most difficult, because this professional is one of the most targeted, not only in Brazil, but worldwide. He is the type of professional who needs, first of all, to be a leader. You have to know how to deal with all kinds of people. A football coach who does not have leadership qualities is doomed to fail or just be one more. A successful coach must know how to exercise a strong leadership model, but without hurting susceptibilities. He must have diplomacy. He cannot be rude. And one of the greatest virtues of a football coach is precisely that of knowing how to give his athletes a reputation for caring. When you give the starter shirt to a player, he is actually throwing a huge responsibility on your back. The coach at this time is showing that he trusts the player and expects him to respond. He is giving something very valuable that he, the player, has to take care of. And the player now has to look after his reputation, his status as a starter.

Luiz Felipe Scolari and Vanderlei Luxemburgo are among the best examples of Brazilian coaches, extremely successful, not only here in Brazil, but also abroad. And, not coincidentally, they can be appointed as excellent conductors of people, exercising a strong type of leadership without losing sight of the psychological aspects, without distancing themselves from the human factor. They know how to praise at the right time, they know how to value their subjects, but they also know how to correct when necessary. And they always have their team in their hands! They are leaders!

Here again we have the combination of several principles already mentioned, such as praising, valuing the person's work, launching challenges etc., but the situation now, the main focus, becomes the attribution of a responsibility, something important for the person and that makes you feel responsible. That's when the person "does his best for the cause", that is, he embraces a cause, a project, a company, a team and assumes a posture of cooperation, of delivery, but always having as background his concern to look after something that he, somehow, sees it as his. He feels that he is an effective part of his group and wants to stay that way, wants to take care of it.

Carlos Batista, a businessman from Orlândia, told us that he applies this principle in his company with great success. Corrects attitudes and directs people with this tool. His staff is small, it is a "lean" company, but highly productive and extremely qualified. He attributes this precisely to that characteristic that predominates in his management, in his leadership style. In their group, everyone acts as if they were partners in the company, this is because each one is responsible for a project, for "his" project and is fully committed to make his system work perfectly. In addition, they show unusual interest in the performance of the company as a whole. They link the success of his individual project to the success of the company. They have a reputation for caring.

## 11. Be polite and firm in commanding the process

> *It doesn't have to be good or bad, it needs to be fair.*

> *Be tough with situations and generous with people.*
> *(Antônio Kock)*

When you are talking to someone who is not very easy to deal with, you need to be polite, but at the same time, to be firm, to be a kind of colonel, you have to be the one who commands. This principle is reminiscent of that other - have command with skill. The difference is that the one applies to command conditions in general and this one is practically the same principle, which we recommend using in situations where we are dealing with difficult people. In this case, what is intended is not to lose the 'pulse', not to lose control of the situation and at the same time not to provoke the "beast". It is a situation that requires a lot of tact. Show who has the power to command and, at the same time, be courteous, be polite, be a diplomat.

To deal with each profile of a difficult person, I present some procedures that, for sure, can do a lot to leave firmly and "whole" out of each situation:

1. To handle dominating and controlling types
   - Neither an eye for an eye nor submission are possible reactions.
   - Show respect without being submissive.
   - Try to show different points of view without attacking directly.
   - Exercise tolerance, even if the other is wrong.

2. To deal with aggressive or harsh people
   - Gentleness is not an adequate posture with subjects of this profile.
   - Confront the behavior clearly, not the person.
   - Look in the eyes and address the other by name.
   - Never humiliate or despise.

- Have the courage to interrupt before things get out of hand.

3. To deal with mistrusting people
    - Satisfy his basic security need.
    - Answer with other questions.
    - Ignore his attacks.
    - Ask if mistrust is always or only in that case.
    - Allow for momentary and calculated "certain lack of intelligence".

4. To deal with silent people
    - Ask more open questions. Avoid the form of an interrogation.
    - Build dialogue bridges.
    - Train patience.
    - Stifle his urge to help by breaking the ice.

5. To deal with super sympathetic people
    - Remember that they are too good to be real.
    - Shut up sympathetically in the face of too many pretensions.
    - Accept apologies without investigating their degree of veracity.
    - Never think that courtship is personal.

- Train the ability to ask selective questions.

6. To deal with martyrs
    - Remember that you need to save your own skin.
    - Listen carefully (without making personal disclosures) in order for the other to release their pent-up emotions.
    - Stop complaints.
    - Focus on the present.
    - Problems must be resolved and not discussed to exhaustion.
    - Question the excessive negative language.

7. To deal with people with a delusion of grandeur
    - Describe the behaviors that must be corrected.
    - Delegate great tasks to him.
    - Escalate these people to teach children to share activities.

8. To deal with pessimists and negativists
    - Never let yourself be infected.
    - Speak slowly.
    - Be patient.

- Ask questions that ask for answers with solutions to difficulties.
- Use the good mood.

9. To deal with the dramatic people
   - Set boundaries through clear articulations.
   - Leave a topic in half and talk about a different subject, after all we have to survive.
   - Never drown in the tsunami of the dramatic.
   - Maintain eye contact and ask what he does differently to change things.

10. To deal with the intolerant
    - Never be intimidated.
    - Interpret them with kindness.
    - Use a touch of irony.
    - Put your limits.
    - Only turn the table over as a last resort.

It is necessary to acquire the habit of using the available instruments according to the requirement of the moment, that is, to know how to use the principles when they are needed. We repeat: they are a toolbox that is always available for you to open and choose the most appropriate for the situation, the one that best applies to a given issue.

Thus, we offer a set of norms, rules, tools that can make you, the reader, a Master of Mind in the art of relationship, in the art of dealing with people, in the art of making friends. This will certainly be a great differentiator for you in the world of business and human relations, and will undoubtedly lead you to a more prosperous, fairer and happier life.

## 12. Conclusion

Dear friend, great winner, remember this motto:

> *The world spins around your thoughts*
> *and changes through your actions.*

What changes the world are not the ideas, but the ideas put into practice. If you've read this book so far, celebrate it. It may seem like little, but you represent a small number. My friend Rogério Silva, on one of our trips to Franca, commented on the large number of people who start a book and do not finish reading.

Many people start and stop in the middle. This is how these people live their lives: settling for half a book, half a victory, half a success, half a happiness, half a smile, half a life. The person who finishes what starts is a winner. You already demonstrate that you are a winner, because you demonstrate your ability to see things complete, to start and end.

Look people in the eye, greet them, call them by name, smile. You are part of a group of people from a generation that is willing to take over this great nation that is Brazil. Celebrate your existence. You are someone who knows the secret of the manual, 'the cat jump'; is versed, from now on, in the art of relationship. Put it into practice. This book was written to be read and reread, until each concept, each principle, each tool is absorbed in its breadth and put into practice.

This book is a Maktub (it is written). On any page you open, it will have a human relations tip for you. Do it bedside.

I know that one day we will meet or meet again somewhere on Earth. If we do not meet, we will still be connected with certainty in the unlimited consciousness that is God.

I hope that one day, when looking back, you will see this moment as a milestone in your life. May life take good care of you, and may God, our Heavenly Father, bless and enlighten you throughout life.

A big and fraternal hug!

Always to the victory!

# BIBLIOGRAPHY

CURY, Augusto. *Inteligência multifocal.* São Paulo: Culrix, 1998.

_____ *Mestre da sensibilidade.* Colina (SP): Academia de Inteligência, 2000. DI STÉFANO, Rhandy. *Manual do sucesso total.* São Paulo: Elevação, 2000. GARDNER, Howard. *Mentes extraordinárias.* Rio de Janeiro: Rocco, 1997.

_____ *Inteligências múltiplas.* Porto Alegre: Artmed, 1978.

HILL, Napoleon. *A lei do triunfo.* Rio de Janeiro: José Olímpio, 1964.

HOUEL, Alane GODEFROY, Christian. *Como lidar com pessoas difíceis.* São Paulo: Madras, 2004.

MUSSAK, Eugênio. *Metacompetência.* São Paulo: Gente, 2003.

SAM, Deep e LYLE, Susman. *Atitudes inteligentes.* São Paulo: Nobel, 1992. SMITH, Steve. *Seja o melhor.* São Paulo: Clio, 2000.

STEPHEN, Covey R. *O oitavo hábito*. Rio de Janeiro: Campus, 2005. THOMAS, Stewart A. *Capital intelectual*. Rio de Janeiro: Campus, 1998. WEOR, Samael Aun. *O matrimônio perfeito*. Editora Instituto Gnóstico de An- tropologia do Brasil.

ZUKER, Elaina. *Influenciar — você também é capaz e talvez não saiba*. São Paulo: Makron Books, 1993.

BOOKS TO CHANGE THE WORLD. YOUR WORLD.

To find out about our upcoming releases
and available titles, visit:

🌐 www.**citadel**.com.br

**f** /**citadeleditora**

📷 @**citadeleditora**

🐦 @**citadeleditora**

▶ Citadel – Grupo Editorial

For more information or questions about the work,
please contact us by email:

✉ contato@**citadel**.com.br